What people are saying about …

A FAREWELL TO MARS

"Brian Zahnd fuses his vocation as prophet and pastor into a powerful evocation of the Prince of Peace, Jesus the Peacemaker. The marvel of his language is that he does this without anger, without pessimism, without a political position, content to simply develop the Jesus agenda while relentlessly exposing the lies and hypocrisies that replace the biblical revelation with a God of War. And the writing is simply brilliant—not a dull sentence in the book."

Eugene H. Peterson, professor emeritus of
Spiritual Theology at Regent College, Vancouver

"Brian Zahnd has written an exceptional book. *A Farewell to Mars* is deeply moving and filled with profound truths about Jesus and the kingdom he proclaimed. Every Christian should read this book."

Adam Hamilton, pastor of the United
Methodist Church of the Resurrection and
author of *When Christians Get It Wrong*

"Pastor Brian troubles me. He will trouble you too, if you dare to read *A Farewell to Mars*. We all need our long-held notions about war and violence to be challenged in the light of what Jesus really taught. I dare you to read this with me."

Brady Boyd, pastor of New Life Church
and author of *Addicted to Busy*

"*A Farewell to Mars* is provocative, prophetic, and pastoral. Zahnd hits it out of the park as he shares his personal journey toward the path of peace. This small book is packed with insight and liberating good news. It is simply the best book I have ever read on Jesus's way of peace."

Michael Hardin, executive director at Preaching
Peace and author of *The Jesus Driven Life*

"How do Christ followers live gently in a violent world? Brian Zahnd, in a powerful, prophetic, and poignant manner, challenges us to wrestle with the revolutionary ideas of Jesus about peace and justice; his desire for his followers is to align themselves around these hope-filled ideas. Make no mistake: the primary focus of Zahnd's book is not peace, but the Prince of Peace. Brian's invitation is not merely to believe in the person of Jesus, but to actually live into the way of Jesus."

J. R. Briggs, cultural cultivator at the
Renew Community, founder of Kairos
Partnerships, and author of *Fail*

"Brian Zahnd is the most truly prophetic preacher in America—an Amos or Micah for our day—with all the usual zealous 'haters' to prove it! And as a wordsmith, Brian writes as he preaches: personally, poetically, passionately. His Christ-centered, cruciform gospel of peace is precisely the wake-up call that the nation needs. Let this word in; let it change you."

Brad Jersak, PhD, faculty of New Testament and Patristics at Westminster Theological Centre (UK)

"When Mars and Christ confront one another, as they often do, those of authentic faith should respond well and wisely to the Prince of Peace. Sadly, many Christians put more faith in the strange god of war than Christ. *A Farewell to Mars* clarifies, in a poignant and evocative manner, what it means to be born again 'toward the biblical gospel of peace.'"

Ron Dart, professor in the Department of Political Science, Philosophy and Religious Studies, University of the Fraser Valley

"Brian Zahnd makes me uncomfortable the way someone who cares confronts you at an intervention. In his incredibly insightful and deeply personal book, Zahnd forces us to face our own, and the church's, destructive attachment to the 'power of the mob' and the 'spirit of war' that often makes us feel righteous when we express it, but takes us far away from the subversive, yet healing, kingdom of Christ. For too long the church has used Jesus as a tool to facilitate salvation instead of following Jesus as our Prince of Peace and Lord of Lords. This book offers the Church a crucial course correction."

Bruxy Cavey, teaching pastor at The Meeting House and author of *The End of Religion*

"Aching with the joy and poetry of repentance, Brian Zahnd beats his pulpit into a plowshare and confesses the excitement of learning to speak a better word than the blood of Abel, a word worthy of the Lamb that was slain. At a time when the message of the cross morphs into a sword and the gospel of peace is sacrificed on the altars of war, I can think of few books from a pastor more important, powerful, and prophetic. Hallelujah!"

Jarrod McKenna, Australian peace award-winning activist, World Vision Advisor, and cofounder of First Home Project

"In this powerful and prophetic book, Brian Zahnd shares his dream—that Christ followers would seek first Christ's dream: a peaceable kingdom full of citizens who believe in, pray for, and work toward a peaceable world. My fear is that many people will see this as an impossible dream and dismiss it as impractical. Sadly, many people thought the same thing about a slaughtered Lamb on a cross. My dream is that lots of people will read this book and allow themselves to be radically transformed by the gospel of peace that it proclaims. My prayer is that, by God's grace, we may believe in Jesus and in his radical ideas of love, forgiveness, and peace."

Joseph S. Beach, pastor at Amazing Grace Church and author of the forthcoming *An Ordinary Church*

"I want to say that this is an 'explosive' book, but such violent imagery simply won't do. This is a healing book, a book that puts things back together again. Drawing richly from biblical texts, theological tradition, and literary beauty, Zahnd offers us a drink from a long-forgotten stream. And if we drink deeply, we may just be part of seeing our world, a wasteland weary from fighting, become a Garden once again."

Glenn Packiam, pastor at New Life Downtown and author of *Discover the Mystery of Faith, Lucky,* and *Secondhand Jesus*

"*A Farewell to Mars* blends biblical clarity and humble vulnerability in a profound and eye-opening manner. This book is right in all the right ways. Right tone, right truth, right timing. With massive guts and even more grace, Brian Zahnd shows how the revolutionary good news of Jesus intersects with our responsibilities as temporary citizens of a superpower. Zahnd is no mere provocateur. He's a prophetic voice. I pray the American church listens."

Evan Wickham, singer/songwriter and worship pastor at Westside: A Jesus Church, Portland, Oregon

"By sharing his own story with remarkable self-effacing honesty, Brian Zahnd masterfully exposes the truth that the church in America has, to a large degree, been preaching a watered-down, thoroughly Americanized gospel. And as Brian demonstrates in this bold and compelling work, the clearest proof of this is that the majority of American Christians fail to see that loving enemies and swearing off violence lies at the heart of everything Jesus was about! This well-written book would wonderfully rock the world of many Christians if they would dare to read it, so I'd like to personally dare them to do so!"

Dr. Gregory Boyd, senior pastor at Woodland Hills Church and author of *Letters from a Skeptic, The Myth of a Christian Nation,* and *God at War*

"*A Farewell to Mars* is the best, most lucid, prophetic, and important book written by any pastor in our times. It is peerless—a book so prophetic in its critique of the forces of empire as to be a work of pastoral treason. Brian Zahnd channels Dylan, Girard, Yoder, Hauerwas, and von Balthasar in a brash, bold pastoral synthesis. *A Farewell to Mars* builds the peaceable kingdom of Jesus up and burns most everything else down. I could not love this deliciously traitorous book more!"

Jonathan Martin, lead pastor at
Renovatus and author of *Prototype*

"This book is brilliant, beautiful, and dangerous!"

Jason Upton, recording artist

A FAREWELL TO MARS

A FAREWELL TO MARS

An Evangelical Pastor's Journey
Toward the Biblical Gospel of Peace

BRIAN ZAHND

David C Cook®

transforming lives together

A FAREWELL TO MARS
Published by David C Cook
4050 Lee Vance View
Colorado Springs, CO 80918 U.S.A.

David C Cook Distribution Canada
55 Woodslee Avenue, Paris, Ontario, Canada N3L 3E5

David C Cook U.K., Kingsway Communications
Eastbourne, East Sussex BN23 6NT, England

The graphic circle C logo is a registered trademark of David C Cook.

Unless otherwise noted, all Scripture quotations are taken from New Revised
Standard Version Bible, copyright © 1989 National Council of the Churches of
Christ in the United States of America. Used by permission. All rights reserved.
Scripture quotations marked ESV are taken from The Holy Bible, English Standard
Version® (ESV®), copyright © 2001 by Crossway, a publishing ministry of Good
News Publishers. Used by permission. All rights reserved; NIV are taken from
Holy Bible, New International Version®, NIV® Copyright © 1973, 1978, 1984,
2011 by Biblica, Inc.® Used by permission. All rights reserved worldwide.
The author has added italics to Scripture quotations for emphasis.

LCCN 2014934629
ISBN 978-0-7814-1118-9
eISBN 978-1-4347-0792-5

© 2014 Brian Zahnd
The Author is represented by the literary agency of Alive
Communications, Inc., 7680 Goddard Street, Suite 200, Colorado
Springs, CO 80920. www.alivecommunications.com.

The Team: John Blase, Amy Konyndyk, Nick Lee, Tonya Osterhouse, Karen Athen
Cover Design: Nick Lee
Cover Photo: Shutterstock

Printed in the United States of America
First Edition 2014

1 2 3 4 5 6 7 8 9 10

032114

For Jude, Mercy, and Finn

Contents

O God, you have made of one blood all the peoples of the earth, and sent your blessed Son to preach peace to those who are far off and to those who are near: Grant that people everywhere may seek after you and find you; bring the nations into your fold; pour out your Spirit upon all flesh, and hasten the coming of your kingdom; through Jesus Christ our Lord. *Amen.*

—*The Book of Common Prayer*

Prelude

Dear Little Book,

I had to write you. You wouldn't let me sleep until you were written. You were rude in your insistence. I had thought I would wait till I was older, till I had less to lose before I wrote you. But then Jude, Mercy, and Finn came along, and you insisted on being written for them. So I did your bidding. Now you are written. Soon you will be let loose to go where you will and speak to whom you may. Try not to cause me too much trouble. At least be kind enough to remind your readers that, in writing you, I only told the truth. I wish you well.

Your Somewhat Reluctant Author,

Brian Zahnd

FOLLOWING THE PRINCE OF PEACE

Though some may contest the point—and I've heard them do so for years—there is something profoundly unsettling about watching those who follow Jesus, the Prince of Peace, use weapons of warfare to kill others and still think they are somehow following Jesus. At the simplest level of evangelicalism—and by that I mean anyone who affirms salvation in Christ alone—it impossible for me to comprehend how a Christian can kill a non-Christian who is thereby prevented from turning to Christ, just as it is also beyond me how any Christian can kill another Christian at the orders of state military leaders. In both instances, the Christian renders to Caesar what is due only to Christ.

As Brian Zahnd says in this aesthetic and courageous book, too often the church—and individual Christians are therefore complicit—has become chaplain to the state. Its divinely ordained and Christ-shaped role is thereby denied; it has become idolatrous and has betrayed the Prince of Peace. Our responsibility is not to chaplain the state but to call the state to repentance and to surrender to the King who is Lord. Our responsibility is to be an alternative to the state. Christians would do far more good for our country by learning not to look to DC for solutions but to the glorious Son of God, who loves us and gave himself for us and, in doing so, gave us a whole new way of life—one not shaped by the power of force but the force of the gospel.

Leaders like Brian Zahnd are quietly becoming more numerous, not because they've turned Euro on us but because they've turned once again to the Gospels and to the New Testament to find an alternative political vision for our world. They've eschewed pragmatics and compromise for a full-throated commitment to the kingdom vision of Jesus, which is necessarily political, but an alternative politic. This alternative political world, which Stanley Hauerwas calls a "peaceable kingdom," refuses to flash the sword of Caesar or Constantine, Germany or the USA, and instead flashes the cross as the way to live. The cross is the symbol of the politics of Jesus, and it is beginning to burn its way into the heart of so many in the church in the USA. We need it.

Particularly in the church in the USA. Why? Because after a century or more of rather simple confusion of the church and state due to the vast majority of Americans calling themselves Christians, or at least being comfortable with a Christian kind of country, Americans woke up to choice in the twentieth century. That century saw the gradual diminution of the church's voice in the public sector and forced some Christians to a kind of activism of taking back what it thought it previously had. But it never had the state. Many thought the church's voice was shaping the state or at least calling it back to its roots, but we have learned that the state had the church by the throat.

It is when the state has the church by the throat that a book like *A Farewell to Mars* suddenly offers clarity. Maybe Brian Zahnd's father is right; maybe the majority *is* almost always wrong.

Scot McKnight
Professor of New Testament
Northern Seminary

CHAPTER I

"THAT PREACHER OF PEACE"

It was my worst sin.

That's what I believe about it. And I deeply believe it. And I'm ashamed of it. But I'm going to tell you about it anyway. This confession is not because I have a penchant for sensational self-deprecation (I don't) but because I want to write honestly. I hope that by telling the truth, what I have to say—especially about my own journey as it pertains to things like war and peace—will carry more weight. Anyway, here's the story.

It was January 16, 1991. I was busy and excited. As the pastor of a rapidly growing nondenominational church, I was busy with all the sorts of things pastors do. But that day, I kept a radio on in my study to stay abreast of the big news: America was going to war! That was what I was excited about. The real fighting of the Gulf War was about to begin—Operation Desert Storm. The bombing of Baghdad. A real shooting war. And it was going to be on TV! That evening I hurried home, so terribly excited. This was going to be a first—a war was on, and CNN would be there to bring it live into my living room! Like the Super Bowl! And that's how I treated it. Friends were invited to the viewing party. We ordered pizza. We watched a war. On TV. America won. CNN had huge ratings. Wolf Blitzer became famous. I was entertained.

I certainly had no qualms about America going to war. That is what America did. America went to war to keep the world "safe for democracy." Saddam Hussein had invaded Kuwait. The UN had passed a resolution. "America's pastor" had prayed with America's president. And anyway, wasn't Iraq the nefarious Babylon of biblical prophecy? Dropping bombs on Babylon had such a powerful apocalyptic appeal that it just *felt* right.

America is always right in war—I'd known that all of my life. Like many Americans, I had grown up believing that war was both inevitable in life and compatible with Christianity. So while America's pastor prayed with America's president in the White House and Wolf Blitzer gave the play-by-play, I ate pizza and watched a war on TV in my living room. It was better than *Seinfeld*!

And I didn't think about it again for fifteen years. I promise you, my pizza-eating, war-watching evening of entertainment didn't cross my mind for fifteen years. Then, one day in 2006, while I was in prayer, for no apparent reason this whole scene from a decade and half earlier played back in my mind. I had forgotten all about it. But there it was, played back in my memory like an incriminating surveillance video. Then I heard God whisper, "That was your worst sin." That whisper was a devastating blow. I wept and repented and wept. Had I been so shallow, so desensitized, so lacking in Christlikeness that I could think of war and violent death as a kind of entertainment? Of course that was part of the problem: televised war carried out by cruise missiles and smart bombs launched from a safe distance seemed like a video game ... except that the points scored were human beings killed.

On the few occasions I have shared this story, there are always those who want to assure me that this could not *possibly* be my worst sin. All I can say is I know the whisper I heard in prayer. But I do find solace in the fact that January 1991 was a long time ago, and I'm no longer that person. How I reached the point where I could weep over war and repent of any fascination with it is part of what this book is about—it's the story of how I left the paradigms of nationalism, militarism, and violence as a legitimate means of shaping the world to embrace the radical alternative of the gospel of peace.

But this book is mostly about Jesus of Nazareth and the revolutionary ideas he preached—especially his ideas about peace. This first-century Jew from whose birth we date our common era, this One who became the heir of Isaiah's ancient moniker Prince of Peace preached a new way of being human and an alternative arrangement of society that he called the reign or kingdom of God. It was (and is!) a peaceable kingdom.

My claim, which I'm told is audacious by some and naive by others, is simply this: Jesus Christ and his peaceable kingdom are the hope of the world. So let me declare from the very beginning: I believe in Jesus Christ! I believe what the canonical gospels report and what the historic creeds confess concerning the crucified and risen Christ. That's what makes me an *orthodox* Christian. But I also believe in Jesus's *ideas*—the ideas he preached about the peaceable kingdom of God. And that's what makes me a *radical* Christian. Believing in the divinity of Jesus is the heart of Christian orthodoxy.

But believing in the viability of Jesus's *ideas* makes Christianity truly radical.

Divorcing Jesus from his ideas—especially divorcing Jesus from his *political* ideas—has been a huge problem that's plagued the church from the fourth century onward. The problem is this: when we separate Jesus from *his* ideas for an alternative social structure, we inevitably succumb to the temptation to harness Jesus to *our* ideas—thus conferring upon our human political ideas an assumed divine endorsement. With little awareness of what we are doing, we find ourselves in collusion with the principalities and powers to keep the world in lockstep with the ancient choreography of violence, war, and death. We do this mostly unconsciously, but we do it. I've done it. And the result is that we reduce Jesus to being the Savior who guarantees our reservation in heaven while using him to endorse our own ideas about how to run the world. This feeds into a nationalized narrative of the gospel and leads to a state-owned Jesus. Thus, our understanding of Christ has mutated from Roman Jesus to Byzantine Jesus to German Jesus to American Jesus, etc. Conscripting Jesus to a nationalistic agenda creates a grotesque caricature of Christ that the church must reject—now more than ever! Understanding Jesus as the Prince of Peace who transcends idolatrous nationalism and overcomes the archaic ways of war is an imperative the church must at last begin to take seriously.

Okay, let's step back and think for a moment about where we stand as a people and a planet. It's easy to imagine that the world doesn't really change—that it simply marches around the maypole of violence, trampling the victims into the mud same as it ever has. But as true as that may be, something *has* changed. We are post*something*. If nothing else, we are post-1945 when the enlightenment dream of attainable utopia went up in smoke—literal smoke!—from the chimneys of Auschwitz and a mushroom cloud over Hiroshima. After 1945 we lost our blind faith in the inevitability of human progress. A threshold was crossed, and something important changed when humanity gained possession of what previously only God possessed: the capacity for complete annihilation. In yielding to the temptation to harness the fundamental physics of the universe for the purpose of building city-destroying bombs, have we again heard the serpent whisper, "You will be like God"? When J. Robert Oppenheimer, the father of the atomic bomb, witnessed the first atomic detonation at Los Alamos on July 16, 1945, he recalled the words of Vishnu from the Bhagavad Gita—"Now I am become Death, the destroyer of worlds." When the monstrous mushroom cloud rose over the New Mexico desert, did the human race indeed become Death, the destroyer of worlds? It's more than a legitimate question. We've now lived for more than a generation with the most haunting post-Holocaust/Hiroshima uncertainty: Can humanity possess the capacity for self-destruction and not resort to it? The jury is still out. But this much is certain—if we think the ideas of Jesus about peace are irrelevant in the age of genocide and nuclear weapons, we have invented an utterly irrelevant Christianity!

Because the stakes are now so intolerably high, people with a modicum of common sense have come to realize we must at last talk seriously about how to live together peaceably on our little blue planet. Our capacity for self-destruction demands this. But people committed to the idea of peace as a real alternative to the paradigms of power and violence often see Jesus and his followers as peripheral to the cause of peace. They don't see the need to get the serious business of peacemaking mixed up with a religious figure—especially when the religion he inspired has so often been associated with violence and war. On the other hand, it too often seems that those who are most committed to the person of Jesus Christ see little need to get Jesus mixed up in the real-world work of peacemaking (which they view as slightly suspicious anyhow). Certainly the evangelical view of real-world peacemaking has been something like this: "Doesn't Jesus have more important work to do?" According to this view, Christianity is mostly about the spiritual work of saving souls for an afterlife in heaven, and Jesus's ideas about peace can be put on hold until the age to come. So the argument goes. But I think otherwise. Jesus Christ and the historical events of his crucifixion and resurrection are not to be separated from the ideas he preached about a kingdom of peace. Or let me say it this way: I believe in the Nazarene who one writer called "that preacher of peace."

In his fascinating novel *The Master and Margarita*, Russian writer Mikhail Bulgakov created an imaginary conversation between the Roman governor Pontius Pilate and the Galilean prophet Yeshua. When asked about his views on government, Bulgakov's Yeshua said, "All power is a form of violence over people." The peasant preacher of Bulgakov's novel went on to contrast the governments of power and violence with the peaceable kingdom of truth and justice. In response Pontius Pilate raged, "There never has been, nor yet shall be a greater or more perfect government in this world than the rule of the emperor Tiberius!"

When Pilate asked Yeshua if he believed this kingdom of truth would come, Yeshua answered with conviction, "It will." Pilate could not and would not stand for this. In a memorable passage, Bulgakov's Pilate railed against the possibility of the kingdom of God ever coming and supplanting Caesar's empire.

> "It will never come!" Pilate suddenly shouted in a voice so terrible that Yeshua staggered back. Many years ago in the Valley of the Virgins Pilate had shouted in that same voice to his horsemen: "Cut them down! Cut them down!" … And again he raised his parade-ground voice, barking out the words so that they would be heard in the garden: "Criminal! Criminal! Criminal! … Do you imagine, you miserable creature, that a Roman Procurator could release a man who has said what you have said to me? … *I don't believe in your ideas!*"[1] (emphasis added)

In *The Master and Margarita*, Bulgakov's Yeshua is a considerably weaker and far less compelling figure than the Jesus of the Gospels. (I find it interesting that literary attempts to depict Jesus Christ always seem to fall far short of what Matthew, Mark, Luke, and John achieved in presenting Jesus as both historically unique and entirely believable.) But I do think Bulgakov gets Pontius Pilate just about right. The pragmatic and occasionally brutal Roman governor belonged to a system of power that had produced the greatest economic and military superpower the world had ever known. Surely an itinerant preacher from a provincial backwater poses no threat to the imperial might of Rome. Yet Pilate *did* see a potential threat in the revolutionary ideas of the Galilean.

It wasn't so much the *man* who upset the Roman governor, but his *ideas*. Pilate understood the nature of ideas. Ideas are powerful, because they are the engines of potential change—and change can be dangerous. When gradual change is perceived as positive and in general keeping with the status quo, we call it *progress*. But radical, paradigmatic change is something else, something more dangerous. We call it *revolution*. Revolutionary change is precisely what those in positions of privilege and power—people like Pilate—are most threatened by. This is why Yeshua and his ideas are perceived as dangerous. In *The Master and Margarita*, Pontius Pilate seems to have no personal animosity toward the wandering Galilean preacher, but Pilate hates his *ideas*. In the end, what forces the procurator to condemn Yeshua to crucifixion is the preacher's revolutionary ideas about power, truth, and violence. If Yeshua had been content to confine himself to the dreamy world of afterlife expectations and had not harbored revolutionary ideas about human social structure, Pilate would have seen little reason to bother with Yeshua, much less crucify him. But Yeshua *did* have revolutionary ideas. And it was Yeshua's ideas about an alternative arrangement of the world—an arrangement that might best be called peace—that resulted in his death by state-sponsored execution.

Anyway, that's how the deal went down in Mikhail Bulgakov's imaginative novel (much of which is in keeping with the narrative we find in John's gospel). A preacher of peace was executed for his revolutionary ideas. But have the ideas of Jesus somehow become less radical since a Roman governor sentenced him to crucifixion during Passover in the spring of AD 30? No. Two thousand years have *not* made the ideas taught by Jesus of Nazareth any less radical than those that so threatened Pontius Pilate and the imperial ideology he was aligned with. What *has* happened over the ensuing two millennia is that we who confess Christ have deftly (and mostly unconsciously) crafted a religion that neatly separates the Jesus who died on the cross for the radical ideas he preached—ideas that Jesus foresaw would lead to his crucifixion.

Jesus always understood that Rome (and the colluding religious powers) would initially refuse to be converted and would crucify him for his ideas. Jesus called these revolutionary ideas "the kingdom of God." Jesus also believed that ultimately the kingdom of God would triumph ... but not through violence.

So here we are, twenty centuries down the road, still wrestling with the conflict we have between the Jesus we love and his unsettling ideas, which we remain skeptical about. It seems we Christians have had a habitual tendency to separate Jesus from his ideas. This bifurcation between Jesus and his political ideas has a history—it can be traced back to the early fourth century when Christianity first attained favored status in the Roman Empire. In October of 312, the Roman general Constantine came to power after winning a decisive battle in which he used Christian symbols as a fetish, placing them as talismans upon the weapons of war. (The incongruence is absolutely stunning!) Having emerged victorious in a Roman civil war and securing his position as emperor, Constantine attributed his military victory to the Christian God. In short order, the wheels were set in motion for Christianity to become the state religion of the Roman Empire. The kingdom of God had been eclipsed by Christian empire.

Almost overnight the church found itself in a chaplaincy role to the empire and on a trajectory that would lead to the catastrophe of a deeply compromised Christianity. The catastrophe of church as vassal to the state would find its most grotesque expression in the medieval crusades when, under the banner of the cross, Christians killed in the name of Christ. The crusades are perhaps the most egregious example of how distorted Christianity can become when we separate Christ from his ideas. Yet we continue to do this—we worship Jesus as Savior while dismissing his ideas about peace. For seventeen centuries Christianity has offered a gospel where we can accept Jesus as our personal Savior while largely ignoring his ideas about peace, violence, and human society. We have embraced a privatized, postmortem gospel that stresses Jesus dying for our sins but at the same time ignores his political ideas. This leaves us free to run the world the way it has always been run: by the power of the sword. Under pressure from the ideology of empire, concepts like freedom and truth gain radically different meanings than those intended by Christ. Freedom becomes a euphemism for vanquishing (instead of loving) enemies; truth finds its ultimate form in the will to power (expressed in the willingness to kill). This is a long way from the ideas of peace, love, and forgiveness set forth by Jesus in the Sermon on the Mount.

It was Jesus's ideas about truth and freedom that made him dangerous to the principalities and powers. But today our gospel isn't very dangerous. It's been tamed and domesticated. If Jesus of Nazareth had preached the paper-thin version of what passes for the "gospel" today—a shrunken, postmortem promise of going to heaven when you die—Pilate would have shrugged his shoulders and released the Nazarene, warning him not to get mixed up in the affairs of the real world. But that's not what happened. Why? Because Pilate was smart enough to understand that what Jesus was preaching *was* a challenge to the philosophy of empire (or as we prefer to call it today, superpower). In making Christ the chaplain-in-chief of Constantinian Christianity, what was unwittingly done was to invent a Manichean Jesus who saves our souls while leaving us free to run the affairs of the world as we see fit.

Which is what we want—especially if the present arrangement of the world has our own particular nation situated near the top. Because while we believe in Jesus as Savior of the private soul, we remain largely unconvinced about his ideas for saving the world. Certainly seventeen centuries of church history strongly suggest this is the case. American Christians especially should keep in mind that we as the modern Romans—the privileged citizens of the world's lone superpower—have more in common with Pontius Pilate than we do with Galilean peasants. Commenting on this, Miroslav Volf says:

> Pilate deserves our sympathies, not because he was a good though tragically mistaken man, but because we are not much better. We may believe in Jesus, but we do not believe in his ideas, at least not his ideas about violence, truth, and justice.[2]

This is how the wheels came off: once it was decided a Christian emperor wielding a "Christian sword" was a suitable way to run the world, the kingdom of God announced by Christ got relocated to a distant heaven or a far-off future, leaving Jesus out of a job as Savior of the world. Of course Constantinian Christianity couldn't quite get away with simply dismissing Christ himself, so he was given the reduced role of saving souls and presiding over a religion of private piety. This is not to suggest that Christ isn't the source of salvation of the human soul, but I *am* suggesting that the mission of Christ extends far beyond the narrow spectrum of private spirituality and afterlife expectations. Jesus actually intends to save the world! And by *world*, I mean God's good creation and God's original intent for human society.

In short the problem is this: far too few who believe in the risen Christ actually believe in his revolutionary *ideas*. There is a sense in which we create religion *as a category* to keep Jesus from meddling with our cherished ideas about nationalism, freedom, and war.

Near the end of the chapter entitled "Pontius Pilate" in *The Master and Margarita*, Bulgakov creates a brilliant imagined conversation between the Roman governor Pilate and the high priest Caiaphas. These two power brokers—one political, one religious—held thinly veiled contempt for one another, but they needed each other to maintain their positions of power. As the story goes, Pilate had two notable prisoners who were both condemned to die. Yeshua Ha-Notsri (Jesus of Nazareth) and Bar-Abba (Barabbas). Pilate asked Caiaphas which prisoner should be granted a Passover pardon and which prisoner should be executed. Caiaphas was presented with a stark choice. The prisoner Bar-Abba was a heroic freedom fighter willing to lead the Jewish people in a war of independence. He had already killed a Roman sentry and represented the national hope of political freedom through violent revolution. Yeshua, on the other hand, was a messiah preaching the revolutionary idea of the peaceable kingdom of God founded upon love and forgiveness. The governor warned the high priest to choose wisely. Without hesitation Caiaphas gave Pilate his answer: "The Sanhedrin requests the release of Bar-Abba." The Sanhedrin had made its choice: they wanted a violent messiah, not a peaceful messiah. But with prophetic insight, Bulgakov's Pilate foretells what will be the inevitable result of Jerusalem choosing the violent Bar-Abba over the peaceful Yeshua:

> Remember my words, High Priest: you are going to see more than one cohort here in Jerusalem! Under the city walls you are going to see the Fulminata legion at full strength and Arab cavalry too. Then the weeping and lamentation will be bitter! Then you will remember that you saved Bar-Abba and you will regret that you sent that preacher of peace to his death![3]

Bulgakov's fictional Pilate foretold what we know as historic reality. A generation after the crucifixion of Christ, Jerusalem finally got its long-awaited war of independence ... and ended up in a smoldering Gehenna. Forty years after the crucifixion, Jerusalem was cast into the hell of Roman siege warfare with the brutal bombardment of one-hundred–pound "hailstones" launched from

Roman catapults, and the final, fiery destruction of the city resulted in the violent death of most of its citizens and the enslavement of the rest.

Unlike Bulgakov's novel, in the Gospels it's Jesus, not Pilate, who foresees this looming disaster. This is why Jesus, as he entered Jerusalem at the beginning of Passover week, lamented the tragic fate of a people who had rejected his way of peace. Luke recorded the event like this:

> As he came near and saw the city, he wept over it, saying, "If you, even you, had only recognized on this day the things that make for peace! But now they are hidden from your eyes. Indeed, the days will come upon you, when your enemies will set up ramparts around you … and your children within you, and they will not leave within you one stone upon another; because you did not recognize the time of your visitation from God. (Luke 19:41–44)

First-century Jerusalem rejected the Prince of Peace and suffered an unspeakable fate—the "city of peace" became a smoking ruin "where their worm never dies, and the fire is never quenched" (Mark 9:48). Their horrible fate could have been avoided, but only if they were willing to renounce the paradigm of violence and see the world through the new paradigm offered by "that preacher of peace." Sadly, they clung to the old lie. And not one stone was left upon another. Jesus's sad prophecy was fulfilled. The charred stones of the first-century ruins in Jerusalem bear witness to the calamity to this day. In rejecting the Prince of Peace, Jerusalem had gone to hell. This was the tragic consequence.

So what about us? Will we fare any better? Do we recognize the things that make for peace? Do we recognize the visitation from God in the life and message of Immanuel? Do we dare to believe in that Prince of Peace who longs to lead humanity into his peaceable kingdom?

I fear we do not. Not most of us. Not most of the time. It seems we, too, have these things hidden from our eyes. We simply cannot envision the world other than it is. Our very imaginations have been commandeered by the principalities and powers. As Walter Brueggemann describes our situation, "Our culture is competent to implement almost anything and to imagine almost nothing."[4]

Here we are twenty centuries after Caiaphas who, for the sake of his nation, and Pilate who, for the sake of his empire, condemned "that preacher of peace" to death in favor of retaining the status quo of violent revolution and militaristic empire. And where are we? Wars continue to define us. Freedom remains a euphemism for the power to kill. Violence is still viewed as a legitimate way of shaping our world. All in an outright betrayal of Jesus Christ and his revolutionary ideas.

But …

I still have hope. Why? Because of the way the Jesus story is told. On Good Friday, the procurator of superpower ideology and the priests of colluding religion rejected his ideas. He was condemned, sentenced, tortured, executed, pronounced dead, and buried in a tomb bearing the imperial seal of Rome. Strike up another victory for the Empire. The End. Yet that's not the end of the story …

On Easter Sunday, the ideas of that preacher of peace
were vindicated by the power of resurrection!

Yes! Easter Sunday and the resurrection of Jesus changed everything! If Jesus had remained in the tomb with its stone sealed by the imperial authority of Rome, Jesus's ideas would have died with him. But the resurrection changes all of that. The resurrection is not only God's vindication of his Son; it is the vindication of all Jesus taught. Easter Sunday is nothing less than the triumph of the peaceable kingdom of Christ. Easter changes everything. Easter is the hope of the world, the dawn of a new age, the rising of the New Jerusalem on the horizon of humanity's burned-out landscape. Easter is God saying once again, "This is my beloved Son, with whom I am well pleased. Listen to him!"

Isn't it time we abandoned our de facto agreement with Pontius Pilate, Caiaphas, and their worn-out, death-dealing ideas? Isn't it time we took seriously the revolutionary, life-giving ideas of Jesus—the one whom God raised from the dead and declared to be Lord by the power of an indestructible life? Isn't it time we were converted and became as children, having the capacity to imagine the radical otherness of the kingdom of God? Isn't it time for the stranglehold of the status quo to give way to the possibilities of prophetic imagination? Isn't it time for the peaceable kingdom of Christ to be considered a viable option in the here and now and not forever relocated to the "sweet by-and-by"? At the very least, we ought to take a fresh look and evaluate with new eyes what Jesus of Nazareth actually taught about the dark foundations of human civilization and the alternative he offers in the kingdom of God. Instead of reading the Gospels through the lens of Constantinian Christianity, where Jesus's prophetic critique of violent power is filtered out, we should try to refamiliarize ourselves with the revolutionary ideas that belong to "that preacher of peace." The American church especially could benefit greatly from an unvarnished reading of Jesus liberated from the censoring lens of militaristic empire and its chaplaincy religion. This book is my attempt to do that.

At this point you may be thinking, *I can't do this. I can't rethink everything I've ever believed about patriotism and war and freedom and manifest destiny and "God bless America."* Sure you can. I did. It may not be easy, but it's not that hard either—as long as you are willing to reexamine everything in the light of Christ.

Once you extricate Jesus from subservience to a nationalistic agenda, you can rethink everything in the light of Christ. And isn't that required of a Christian? I first started thinking this way while reading Fyodor Dostoevsky's prophetic novel, *Demons*. (I call it prophetic, because in it Dostoevsky seems to foresee with terrifying clarity the dark and bloody fate that would fall upon Russia with the rise of Soviet Communism.) In an important passage, Shatov explains to Stavrogin how all great nations believe that God is expressly *their* God—that somehow great nations deify and personify their nation *as* God. I still remember when I first read this passage.

> I raise the nation up to God. Has it ever been
> otherwise? The nation is the body of God. Any
> nation is a nation only as long as it has its own

particular God and rules out all other gods in the world with no conciliation; as long as it believes that through its God it will be victorious and will drive all other gods from the world. ... A truly great nation can never be reconciled with a secondary role in mankind, or even with a primary, but inevitably and exclusively with the first. Any that loses this faith is no longer a nation. But the truth is one, and therefore only one among the nations can have the true God.[5]

That brief passage from a nineteenth-century Russian novel may not move you, but when I read those words for the first time, it so shocked me, I left my house, book in hand, and walked for a mile pondering what I had just read. It was a "take the red pill" moment for me. What I saw was that great and powerful nations shape God into their own image; great and powerful nations conscript God to do their bidding. Great and powerful nations use the idea and vocabulary of God to legitimize their own agenda. Great and powerful nations project God as a personification of their own national interests. And for the most part, they don't know they are doing it. This is not to say that everything great and powerful nations do is evil—far from it. They maintain order, provide security, produce industry, maintain civility, educate the populace, preserve culture, and so on. But neither are they to be confused with the kingdom of Christ. And neither can they claim that the God revealed in the crucified and risen Christ is *their* God, committed to *their* interests! No! There are no "Christian nations" in the political sense. The risen Christ *does* have a "nation" (see Matt. 21:43), but it's not a nationalized body politic, rather it's the baptized body of Messiah! This is what I was beginning to see—disturbing yet liberating truth. It's strange how a novel could crack open my worldview in a way that let the light of truth in, but that's exactly what happened.

In August 2008, my wife, Peri, and I were on our annual summer vacation in the Rocky Mountains. During our vacation, it seemed that with every hike, my mind was absorbed with this idea—that great and powerful nations try to use God to sponsor their agenda and especially their agenda pertaining to violence, war, and their place in the world. This is the modus operandi of the Gentile nations that the Hebrew prophets constantly critiqued. It's not that God is opposed to nations—he's not. God has appointed the nations with their rich diversity and unique cultures. Nations are essential for how a person becomes a person with a particular language, identity, and culture. What God is opposed to, and has always been opposed to, is empire—rich and powerful nations that believe they have a divine right to rule other nations and a manifest destiny to shape the world according to their agenda. God is opposed to the agenda of empire for this simple reason: God makes the same claim for his Son! God has made his Son the true, present, and eternal emperor of the world. With their nationalistic agendas the empires of this age make themselves a rival to Christ. This is never more clear than in the area of violence. Empires believe they have a right to shape the world according to their agenda and that violence is a legitimate means of attaining these ends. Christ clearly rejects this. René Girard says it like this:

Violence is the enslavement of a pervasive lie; it imposes upon men a falsified vision not only of God but also of everything else. And that is indeed why it is a closed kingdom. Escaping from violence is escaping from this kingdom into another kingdom, whose existence the majority of people do not even suspect. This is the Kingdom of love, which is also the domain of the true God, the Father of Jesus, of whom the prisoners of violence cannot even conceive.[6]

Girard is certainly right when he says the majority of people don't even suspect the existence of a kingdom that is sustained by the love of God and operates without violence. It was these kinds of thoughts that dominated my thinking after Dostoevsky acted as my Morpheus and gave me the red pill, enabling me to see the matrix of violent empire. I wrestled with these thoughts as I hiked many a mile through the Rocky Mountains in August 2008. As we drove across Nebraska on the long drive home, a phrase kept running through my mind: *I glimpsed this truth out of the corner of my eye.* It just kept repeating. *I glimpsed this truth out of the corner of my eye.* Finally I pulled over and asked Peri to drive. I grabbed a pen and a legal pad and wrote a subversive and dangerous poem about what I had seen. When I read it to Peri, she said, "You're not going to share this with anyone, are you?"

I said, "Of course not."

I lied.

But that wasn't the worst sin I ever committed.

OUT OF THE CORNER OF MY EYE

I think I caught a glimpse of truth
out of the corner of my eye.
A ghost, a whisper, a suspicion, a
subtle and subversive rumor.
So dangerous that every army would be
commanded to march against it;
so beautiful that it would drive
those who see it to madness
or sanity.
Does the whole of my kind suffer
from mental and moral vertigo?
As Melville said of cabin boy Pip,
he saw the foot of God upon
the treadle of the loom
and dared to speak it.
Henceforth his shipmates called him mad.
As Vladimir said when they came to bury Fyodor,
the spiritual leader must feel the
falsehood prevailing in society;
the prophet must struggle against it,
never tolerate it, never submit to it.
I think I caught a glimpse of truth
out of the corner of my eye.
Have we been so blinded by the
bright lights of advertisers' lies
that the only true vision is peripheral vision?

In the age of constant commercialization
and overblown hype,
does truth shout with a whisper
and stand out with subtlety?
I think I caught a glimpse of truth
out of the corner of my eye.
It terrified me as I fell in love with it.
I said,
This explains everything.
This changes everything.
This challenges everything.
This threatens everything.
This transforms everything.
Dare I speak it?
The truth I caught out of the corner of my eye?
Every empire of man is built upon a lie;
they come to kill, steal, and destroy.
Every empire of man is built upon a lie;
all virtue is subject to sacrifice upon
the altar of imperial expediency.
Every empire of man is built upon a lie;
God or gods exist only to serve its cause.
Every empire of man is built upon a lie;
religion takes off its mask when it says—
We have no king but Caesar.
The ultimate betrayal,
the final apostasy,
every empire of man is built upon a lie.

Marx was more than half right when he said—
Religion is the opiate of the masses.
Every empire of man is built upon a lie:
Self-promotion and Self-preservation,
Greed and Lust,
Industry and War,
the industry of war.
Long live the Empire!
Keep the Empire alive,
and to keep the Empire alive
many will be made to die,
because the Empire lives by the sword
and dies by the same.
Every empire of man is built upon a lie.
From Aztec to Zulu,
Egyptian and Ottoman,
Persia and Babylon,
Greece and Rome,
England and—
Now I'm too close to home.
A kinder, gentler Babylon to be sure,
but a Babylon for sure.
Every empire of man is built upon a lie.
So when Christ came
he did not bring
another empire of men
built upon a lie
as the liar in the desert tempted.

Instead he brought
the Empire of God,
Good News!
The government of justice and
mercy, grace and truth,
and the truth is
every empire of man is built upon a lie,
though every empire says,
We have God on our side.
So you will have to decide
how patriotic a Byzantine believer can be.
May we be salt and light,
a prophetic voice,
a Christian conscience.
May we preserve and illuminate,
cry aloud and convict,
but never forget
every empire of man is built upon a lie.
And to stand for truth
and to stand for God
is to stand against the lie the empire is built upon.
And in the midst of imperial
self-justification pray—
Thy Empire come.
There, I've said it.
The truth I glimpsed out of the corner of my eye.
And when push comes to shove,
as it always does,

the Empire of Men will oppose

the Empire of God.

To know this is dangerous.

To say it can be deadly.

Do you think I'm kidding?

What crucified Jesus?

Self-righteous religion?

No, not religion alone.

Religion as the whore of Empire.

This is what killed Jesus.

And Paul.

And Peter.

And Polycarp.

And Huss.

And Bonhoeffer.

Because this is what empires do.

Silence the prophets who will

not prostitute the truth.

Religion is tolerated.

Imperial religion is promoted.

But the prophetic hope of *another way*

must be censored

even by the sword.

This is the way of empire.

Because

every empire of man is built upon a lie.

Constantine can become a Christian,

but Constantine cannot baptize the Empire.

The Empire of God converts the

hearts of men one at a time.

Christ the King must himself sponsor

each one into his Kingdom.

But when the Empire sanctions

religion for its own purposes,

the whore of Babylon rides the back of the beast.

Giddyup and God bless the Empire!

Every empire of man is built upon a lie.

I glimpsed this truth out of the corner of my eye.

To believe this truth will set you free.

And you thought it was just

Sunday school banality

or empty religious sentimentality

to pray

Thy Empire come

Thy Policy be done.

You had no idea it was dissident and subversive,

because every empire of men is built upon a lie.

The lie that the empire has God on its side.

I glimpsed this truth out of the corner of my eye.

And if you ask me my politics, I will say,

Jesus is Lord!

I glimpsed this truth out of the corner of my eye.

CHAPTER 2

REPAIRING THE WORLD

As the story is told, Peter Pan had a happy thought that enabled him to fly. I have a happy thought too. And if it doesn't exactly enable me to fly, it does give my mind enough buoyancy to untether my imagination from the leaden weights of pessimism. My happy thought is this confession: *Jesus is the Savior of the world*. Your reaction to my happy thought is probably ho-hum. You say, "Well, of course. You're a Christian; you're a pastor." I understand that response. But stick with me and try to understand what I'm saying. The thought that makes me so happy is that Jesus is the Savior of *the world!* This world that you and I inhabit—where we go to work, do our living, raise our children, and try to find meaning and happiness—Jesus is the Savior of *that!* Jesus is not a heavenly conductor handing out tickets to heaven. Jesus is the carpenter who repairs, renovates, and restores God's good world. The divine vision and original intention for human society is not to be abandoned, but saved. That's a big deal! It's the gospel! And it makes me happy!

But this hasn't always been the way I understood the gospel. As a zealous American evangelical, I spent plenty of time peddling "the

bus ride to heaven" reduced version of the gospel. I can tell you it's
a pretty easy sell. You promise the moon (actually heaven) for the
low one-time cost of a sinner's prayer. How hard is that? And since
it mostly applies to the next life, why *wouldn't* you pray the prayer?
If for no other reason than as a kind of afterlife insurance. Oh, yes,
we did offer the optional discipleship package for those wanting to
upgrade their Christian experience. But the important thing was
to fill up the bus for the postmortem ride to heaven. That's largely
how I understood and preached the gospel. And, yes, at times it did
seem a little cheap. But plenty of people made decisions and prayed
the prayer. As the saying goes, you can't argue with the numbers.
(Actually you *can* argue with the numbers—that's what prophets do
all the time.)

Eventually I reached a crisis point concerning what the gospel is and how it should be preached. To a large extent, this came
about when I began to seriously read the apostolic sermons found
in the book of Acts. I had to admit the apostles did *not* preach
the gospel the way I was preaching it. ("Pray the sinner's prayer so
you can go to heaven when you die.") In fact, in the eight gospel
sermons found in the book of Acts, not one of them is based on
afterlife issues! Instead they proclaimed that the world now had a
new emperor and his name was Jesus! Their witness was this: the
Galilean Jew, Jesus of Nazareth, had been executed by Roman crucifixion, but God had vindicated him by raising him from the dead.
The world now had a new boss: Jesus the Christ. What the world's
new Lord (think *emperor*) is doing is saving the world. This *includes*
the personal forgiveness of sins and the promise of being with the
Lord in the interim between death and resurrection as well as after

the resurrection, but the whole project is much, much bigger than that—the world is to be *repaired*! Now *that* is a gospel I can get excited about! A gospel that isn't reserved for the sweet by-and-by, but a gospel that is for the here and now!

Taken seriously this is a bold claim (and among skeptics a debatable one): *Jesus is the Savior of the world*. But this is what our Christian Scriptures tell us. (Explicitly in John 4:42 and 1 John 4:14, and in other ways throughout the entire New Testament.) Yet for that thought to make us happy enough to soar above the dismal status quo, it has to be liberated from the emaciated world of trite religious cliché. If what we mean by "Jesus saves the world" gets reduced to "saved people go to heaven when they die," then Jesus is simply the one who saves us *from* the world, not the Savior *of* the world. But this is *not* what the apostle John meant when he spoke of Jesus as the Savior of the world. John was talking about something much bigger and much more expansive than individuals "accepting Jesus as their personal Savior." John (and the rest of the apostolic writers of the New Testament) presented Christ as the Savior of God's good creation and the restorer of God's original intention for human society. This is the gospel! This is the apostolic gospel, and it's a gospel that gives us an eschatology of hope. By *eschatology of hope*, I mean a Christian vision for the future that is redemptive and not destructive—more anticipating the New Jerusalem and less obsessed with Armageddon.

In our anxiety-ridden world, who can doubt that we desperately need an eschatology of hope? But in order to claim that our Christian message is "good news," we must honestly believe that we are headed for something that is ultimately hopeful. Christian happiness is based in the conviction that because of the accomplishments of Christ, the future is a friend. Without an anticipated end that justifies God's act of creation itself, happiness is mostly a form of escapist fantasy. And faith should never be confused with fantasy. With this in mind let me introduce you to a Jewish scholar and rabbi who insisted that an eschatology of hope is required of those who confess faith in God. His name is Emil Fackenheim, and he came to embrace an eschatology of hope in direct response to the Holocaust.

November 9, 1938, is registered in the catalog of human crimes as Kristallnacht—the Night of Broken Glass. On that dreadful night, when Nazi storm troopers smashed, ransacked, burned, and destroyed Jewish homes, synagogues, and businesses throughout Germany, Emil Fackenheim was among the thirty thousand Jewish men arrested and taken to concentration camps. Through a merciful twist of fate, the twenty-two-year-old Fackenheim managed to escape the Sachsenhausen concentration camp and was eventually able to get out of Nazi Germany. Following the war he made his way to Canada where he became a prominent Jewish philosopher and Reform rabbi. In 1982 Fackenheim wrote *To Mend the World*, an influential book on post-Holocaust Jewish thought. The title comes from the Jewish theological concept of *tikkun olam*—"repairing the world." *Tikkun olam* is the idea that although the world is broken, it is not beyond repair—that it's God's intention to work through humanity in order to repair his creation.

In *To Mend the World*, Emil Fackenheim famously dares to issue to the Jewish community a "614th Commandment." It's an audacious proposition. As far back as the medieval scholar Maimonides, Jewish rabbis have spoken of the Torah containing 613 commandments. But precisely because of the enormity of the Holocaust experience, Fackenheim tells his fellow Jews they must now add one more law to their ancient Torah—a 614th commandment. Commandment 614 is simply this: Thou shalt not give Hitler any posthumous victories. Elaborating on the 614th Commandment, Fackenheim says, "We are forbidden to despair of the world as the place which is to become the kingdom of God, lest we help make it a meaningless place in which God is dead or irrelevant and everything is permitted."[1] Fackenheim was saying to his own Jewish community that even in the face of the Holocaust, they are not permitted to give up on the world; despite all the atrocities, they must continue to believe that a horribly broken world can be repaired. Fackenheim rightly insists that this world is to be the kingdom of God and to despair of this is to collude with wickedness and give vanquished pathogens of evil posthumous victories.

Of course *tikkun olam* is properly a Jewish concept, but it is a Jewish concept that Christians can and should embrace. A Christian understanding of *tikkun olam* is that God is restoring all things through Jesus Christ.[2] And while it may be true that the Jewish community in general has not recognized that God is repairing the world through Jesus, Christians often fail to recognize that God is repairing the world at all! The Jewish failure to embrace Jesus as the restorer of the world is explainable, at least in part, due to the long, sad history of Christian anti-Semitism, pogroms, and persecutions. But the Christian failure to embrace Jesus as the restorer of the world lacks any justification. Nevertheless, whole segments of the church seem to have no idea that God actually intends to save the world. Somewhere along the way, we picked up the inexcusable idea that God has given up on the world. This is especially true in certain forms of world-denying fundamentalism.

Far too many American Christians embrace a faulty, half-baked, doom-oriented, hyperviolent eschatology, popularized in Christian fiction (of all things!), that envisions God as saving parts of people for a nonspatial, nontemporal existence in a Platonic "heaven" while kicking his own good creation into the garbage can! Framed by this kind of world-despairing eschatology, evangelism comes to resemble something like trying to push people onto the last chopper out of Saigon. But this is an evangelism that bears no resemblance to the apostolic gospel proclaimed in the book of Acts. Christianity's first apostles evangelized, not by trying to sign people up for an apocalyptic evacuation, but by announcing the arrival of a new world order. The apostles understood the kingdom of God as a new arrangement of human society where Jesus is the world's true King. Put simply: because Jesus is Lord, the world is to be redeemed and not left in ruin.

The appropriate response to this gospel proclamation is to rethink everything in the light of the risen and ascended Christ and live accordingly. We rethink our lives (which is what it means to repent) not so we can escape a doomed planet, but in order to participate in God's design to redeem the human person and renovate human society in Christ. Salvation is a restoration project, not an evacuation project! Or as Thomas Merton put it, "Eschatology is not an invitation to escape into a private heaven: it is a call to transfigure the evil and stricken world."[3]

That the present world stands in need of renovation is blatantly obvious. Of course. This is nothing new. The world of human civilization has been in trouble for a long time … a *really* long time—it seems from the very beginning. The Bible tells the story of humanity going wrong from the first. A transgression in the garden led to an expulsion from paradise, culminating in brother killing brother and a world addicted to violence. This is the story of Adam and Eve, Cain and Abel, and the violence-drenched days of Noah. It's also the story the Bible tells in the rise of the militaristic empires of Egypt, Assyria, and Babylon, and the envisioned alternative of a kingdom of peace and justice set forth by the Hebrew prophets.

Interestingly, anthropology tells a similar story (at least in part). Anthropologists tell us that the rise of human civilization was made possible largely through the harnessing of agriculture. But this also resulted in the unleashing of violence and the birth of the organized violence we call war. Agriculture-based civilization was a double-edged sword. Cultivating crops allowed for settled and larger communities that gave rise to greater technology and richer culture. Written language originally developed as a means of recording grain stores. But then, it could also be used to record everything from science to sonnets, enriching the whole spectrum of human culture. Unfortunately there is also a dark side. An agriculture-based economy introduced the new concept of land ownership, and once land could be owned, it could be coveted and fought over. This propelled civilization down the road to tribalistic social structure. Civilization advanced by treading upon the corpses of those who were "not us" and "not on our side." This was especially true as conflict arose between the settled agriculture communities and the nomadic shepherding communities who had differing understandings of land (which is one way of understanding the Cain and Abel story). In the Bible the genesis of homicide is told like this: Cain, the tiller of the ground, met his sheep-tending brother, Abel, in a field. Was there a dispute over land? Cain killed his brother and then lied to God (and himself) about what he had done. After the murder Cain ventured east of Eden to build the first city. There you have it—human civilization founded in murder. And the rest is history. Literally.

Humanity's worst sins and most heinous crimes occur when we follow the way of Cain as the founder of human civilization and refuse to recognize the shared humanity of our brothers and fail to acknowledge our responsibility to be our brother's keeper. When vicious competition and blind commitment to tribalism become more valued than the brotherhood of shared humanity, we let Satan loose in our midst. When we denigrate those of differing nationalities, ethnicities, religions, politics, and classes to a dehumanized "them," we open the door to deep hostility and the potential for unimaginable atrocities. If we believe the lie that they are "not like us," we are capable of becoming murderers and monsters. And it's been going on for a long, long time.

In 1991 two hikers in the Italian Alps stumbled upon a 5,300-year-old corpse that would later be dubbed "Ötzi the Iceman." Preserved for more than five millennia in the ice and dry mountain air, Ötzi is the oldest intact corpse ever found. Forensic investigation revealed that Ötzi was most likely a shepherd. Ötzi was also a murder victim. He had been shot in the back with an arrow. As a Bronze Age shepherd who became a murder victim, we might think of Ötzi as the Abel of the Alps. I find it poignant and sadly apropos that the oldest human corpse was not found resting in a peaceful grave with attendant signs of reverence, but sprawled upon a bleak mountainside with an arrow in his back. It's a distressing commentary on the origins of human civilization. It seems that human civilization is incapable of advancing without shooting brothers in the back. From the lonely death of Ötzi in the Italian Alps to Neda Agha-Soltan in Iran, whose violent death in Tehran during the 2009 election protests was captured on a cell-phone camera and witnessed around the world, the number of Abels who lay slain by a Cain are incalculable. In a world that spills the blood of the innocent, it's easy to despair. But it's the world Abel, Ötzi, and Neda were slain in that Jesus came to save.

Yet it is the very claim that Jesus is the Savior of the world (in ways beyond the interiorized realm of private religion) that invites incredulity. The skeptic (or maybe even the Christian) will say, "But just look at the world! How has Jesus made the world any different than it's always been?" It's a fair question and one we should tackle head-on. So let's take the question at face value and ponder just how Jesus *has* made the world different from what it's always been.

As the heirs of the Western tradition that has been shaped religiously, culturally, and ethically by Christianity, we may be oblivious to what should be obvious (like a fish unaware of water). It may be that we are so immersed in the influence of Christ that we fail to recognize it. So I propose a thought experiment. Deliberately imagine a twenty-first-century world *without* Christ. Try it. See if you can imagine it. Attempt to envision a world without the birth in Bethlehem. A world without Christmas. A world that C. S. Lewis might describe as "always winter but never Christmas." A world without an Easter. A world without the story of the crucifixion of the Prince of Peace on that Friday we call Good and without his resurrection on that Sunday we call Easter. What would our world look like absent Christmas and Easter? If you don't conjure images that make you shudder, you're not thinking it through.

Our present age without the life of the one who reset the calendar would be, I have no doubt, a kind of hell on earth. It would resemble the world depicted in the now familiar genre in film and literature known as postapocalyptic. This genre was created nearly two hundred years ago but has become increasingly popular since World War II. Mary Shelley is generally credited with pioneering the postapocalyptic genre with her 1826 publication of *The Last Man*. Though she is best known for *Frankenstein* (her book exploring the moral dilemma of science outpacing ethics), this lesser-known work imagines an apocalyptic future in the late twenty-first century when only a handful of people survive. Written in the early nineteenth century, *The Last Man* was largely ignored until the 1960s, which is to say, until the time when people realized that Dr. Oppenheimer's monstrous creation of the atomic bomb—eerily foreshadowed in *Frankenstein*—had made the apocalyptic scenario of *The Last Man* an actual possibility. Mary Shelley's two horror books were coming to life!

In our own time we are most familiar with the postapocalyptic genre through film. You know what I mean: the world imagined as a blighted wasteland populated with a remnant of half-savage survivors following some kind of catastrophic event. *The Day After* and

Mad Max movies from the eighties and, more recently, *The Road* and *The Book of Eli* are cinematic examples.

It appears that there is something in our collective imagination that is darkly aware of the capacity we possess for unprecedented destruction. But while contemporary writers and filmmakers explore the dark *possibility* of a postapocalyptic world, it is entirely feasible that a world without Christmas and Easter would have already crossed the threshold into a postapocalyptic *reality*. And what has saved us? Jesus! Yes, I believe this. Jesus's achievement in giving humanity an ethic of mercy through the incarnation of love has already done much to save the world from the fate of a self-inflicted Gehenna. How? It works like this: once the world came to see Christ's death upon the cross as an act of cosuffering love and an alternative to violent revenge, it introduced a saving grace that helped mitigate man's inhumanity to man. Nothing has done more to confer dignity upon the individual person than the Christian doctrine of the incarnation. If God can become human, then we must reconsider how we treat our fellow humans. The incarnation has, without question, made the world a more humane place by raising the dignity of every individual.

Of course I can hear the skeptics howl! They will point out that the world has seen plenty of atrocities since the advent of Christ. Indeed. But what skeptics often fail to realize is that it is precisely because of Calvary that we call these things *atrocities* and not *normalcy*. Without the life of Christ, would we call massacres and genocides *atrocities*, or would we call them *just the way things are*? Did the pagan world have the ethical resources to produce what has come to be known as "human rights"? Now I'm the one who is skeptical! In the pre-Christian pagan world, what we now call atrocities were largely seen as simply the triumph of the strong over the weak, the way of nature, the way things ought to be.

A world that had never seen a Christmas and never celebrated an Easter would still be a pagan world bereft of compassion for the poor, the sick, the weak, the marginalized, the victimized—the very people Jesus brings out of the shadows through his life and teaching. Jesus further establishes compassion as the way we are to relate to the weak and suffering when he makes our treatment of them the criterion for the final judgment in the parable of the sheep and goats. In that parable Jesus famously said, "as you did it to one of the least of these my brothers, you did it to me" (Matt. 25:40 ESV). Jesus has taught us to see the sick, the poor, the prisoner, and the stranger as *his* brothers … as *our* brothers … as Jesus himself! This is something entirely new. It was not something bequeathed to us by the pagan world. It was not something the pagan world was capable of producing. In the Genesis story, before he moved east of Eden to found human civilization, Cain cynically asked, "Am I my brother's keeper?" This is how Cain justified himself before God. Cain obviously didn't think he was his brother's caregiver. And neither did Pharaoh or Caesar—the heirs of Cain's city. But in reconfiguring the world around love instead of competition, Jesus answered Cain's question with a resounding *yes* … and then said to us, "And here are your brothers; take care of them."

It is naive and historically unwarranted to think that this kind of compassion—care for those least able to contribute to the welfare of the community—would be regarded as a virtue without Jesus Christ. To locate the origin of concern for "human rights" in something like the secular triumph of the French Revolution instead of the sacred triumph of Christ is a poor and pernicious reading of history. David Bentley Hart speaks to this when he says:

> Even the most ardent secularists among us gener-
> ally cling to notions of human rights, economic
> and social justice, providence for the indigent, legal
> equality, or basic human dignity that pre-Christian
> Western culture would have found not so much
> foolish as unintelligible. It is simply the case that
> we distant children of the pagans would not be able
> to believe in any of these things—they would never
> have occurred to us—had our ancestors not once
> believed that God is love, that charity is the founda-
> tion of all virtues, that all of us are equal before
> the eyes of God, that to fail to feed the hungry or
> care for the suffering is to sin against Christ, and
> that Christ laid down his life for the least of his
> brethren.[4]

Jesus has saved the world from the self-centered, brother-denying ethic witnessed in Cain—an ethic that viewed the helpless as undeserving of aid and unworthy of compassion. After all it was the followers of Jesus who pioneered such radical innovations as hospitals, orphanages, leprosariums, almshouses, relief for the poor, and public education. The idea that the world somehow or other would have arrived at an ethical worldview that could produce such charitable practices and institutions *without Christ* is an idea wholly lacking in any evidence. As I point out to secular critics, I know of many St. Jude and St. James hospitals, orphanages, relief agencies, and the like, but I'm still looking for the Nietzsche hospital or the Voltaire children's home. I'm not suggesting that a world reimagined according to mercy captures all of what it means for Jesus to be the Savior of the world … but it's part of it. So the next time you drive past a children's hospital or a free medical clinic or see a relief agency going about its work of compassion, you should see it as an expression of how Jesus saves the world from its uncaring pagan past—a pagan past we need to remember.

What the city of Cain in its Egyptian, Assyrian, Babylonian, Persian, Greek, and Roman expressions excelled at was building an empire by making victims out of those who got in the way. And you can be sure the victims of pagan empires were nameless and faceless victims. Because Cain forgets Abel. Cain forgets that Abel existed, that Abel was human, and most of all Cain forgets that Abel was his brother. So Abel was forgotten—like the Ice Man lying in the Alps with an arrow in his back. This is the very practice that the cross of Christ so thoroughly exposed and shamed. Today the victims of all systems of greed, injustice, and exploitation are given a face—and it is the face of Christ. That Jesus won his kingdom in a way that gives him solidarity with victims everywhere is something that would have been utterly inconceivable to Ramesses the Great, Alexander the Great, or Julius Caesar.

Because Jesus suffered as a victim of ambitious power hiding behind a facade of legitimacy, all victims of ambitious power are now brought into the light. Christ has become their champion. Christ has forever altered the way the world looks at those victimized by the ambitious and powerful. The post-Easter world has come to have an instinctual empathy for the victim. This is something new. This is a phenomenon that never existed before the world began to see the face of Christ in the face of nameless victims. This doesn't mean that principalities and powers no longer victimize, but it does mean that they can no longer do so with impunity—the cross of Christ exposes their exploitation of the innocent as shameful. It's why Orwellian phrases like *collateral damage* are employed as propaganda instead of just saying, "a hundred thousand civilians were killed." Pharaoh and Caesar didn't have to worry much about public sympathy for the hapless victims who ended up with arrows in their backs, but their modern counterparts do. Why? Because Christ has forever changed how we think about victims. This is part of how Jesus repairs the world—by drawing us away from the self-deception that leads to the self-inflicted curse of Cain.

The Advent of Christ and the spread of Christianity has done much to make the world a more humane and livable place by nurturing a concern for the oppressed and bringing to light those confined to a forgotten underclass. This has been well documented, and reminding ourselves of just a few examples will suffice to make the point. The abolition of slavery—wherever and whenever it has occurred—has always drawn its moral authority from Christ. The fall of totalitarianism in Eastern Europe was the result of Christian movements largely inspired by Pope John Paul II. In South Africa Archbishop Desmond Tutu and Nelson Mandela looked to Christ for their ideals of justice and reconciliation that brought about the peaceful end to the racist policies of apartheid. And without Christ, how could humanity ever have produced a Mother Teresa?

In the saint of Calcutta we find a life dedicated to lifting the dying out of the gutters and in their final moments alerting them to the dignity that was always theirs. But it is only Christ who makes a Mother Teresa possible, because it is only Christ who makes the conferral of dignity upon the destitute and dying a cause worthy of a saint. The idea that human dignity is to be accorded to every person no matter their social status is an idea that would be impossible without the life of Christ. This is part of how Jesus repairs the world.

Consider, too, that slavery, totalitarianism, and apartheid have been challenged, and in places overcome, not by Christians who sat back and blithely said, "It's all going to burn," but by Christians who believed that Jesus is Lord *here and now*. Such Christians believe that the program of restoration is already underway. Laboring in the name of Jesus to make the world a better place does not undermine faith in the Second Coming; rather it takes seriously God's intention to repair the world through Christ and anticipates this hope by moving even now in the direction of restoration. This is what it means to be faithful to the kingdom of God even while we await the appearing of Christ and the culmination of our hope.

Tikkun olam. Repairing the world. Healing wastelands. Laboring to make a dying world livable again. This is the vision of the apostles and prophets. This is the prophetic paradigm the people of God are to coordinate their theology and lives with. We are not to be macabre Christians lusting for destruction and rejoicing at the latest rumor of war. It's high time that a morbid fascination with a supposed unalterable script of God-sanctioned–end-time–hyperviolence be once and for all left behind.

A secret (or not-so-secret) longing for the world's violent destruction is grossly unbecoming to the followers of the Lamb. We are not hoping for Armageddon; we are helping build New Jerusalem. We will not complete it without the return of the King, but we will move in that direction all the same. We refuse to conspire with the beasts of empire who keep the world confined to the death culture of Babylon. There's always another Armageddon looming on the horizon, threatening to perpetuate the bloody ways of Cain and throw more Abels in a mass grave. But we are not to cooperate with that vision. We are to resist it. We are to anticipate a future created by the Prince of Peace through the very lives we live. We are to work in concert with Jesus Christ as he labors to repair the world. Yes, *tikkun olam*!

CHAPTER 3

CHRIST AGAINST THE CROWD

My father was a wise man. He was a judge, deeply respected in the community, known for his integrity, kindness, and wisdom. People said he reminded them of Atticus Finch—the quietly heroic lawyer in *To Kill a Mockingbird*. Like Jem and Scout in Harper Lee's classic novel, I had the great fortune to be raised by a deeply principled man. Among the important things my dad taught me was this jewel of counterintuitive wisdom: the majority is almost always wrong. I remember him saying that to me on many occasions. It was a warning to be suspicious of the crowd, to not trust the crowd, to resist going along with the crowd. My father, as a judge and a man of politics, knew that one of the responsibilities of a just democracy is to protect the minority from the majority. And why? Because the majority is not as interested in truth as it is in power—and power in the hands of a crowd is often used for revenge and scapegoating. The disturbing truth is that a crowd can too easily become a lynch mob, whether literally or metaphorically.

Of course lynch mobs never think of themselves as such—instead they imagine they are simply good people committed to truth and justice, taking a stand against a great evil. The crowd is incapable of entertaining the idea that *it* may be a great evil. Evil *must* masquerade as good; it's the only disguise it can use … so that's what it does. "Even Satan disguises himself as an angel of light" (2 Cor. 11:14 ESV). Crowds never think they are doing evil. But then, crowds are easily duped. Crowds are not wise. Crowds don't think. Crowds only react … usually to fear. That's when bad things happen. We don't need more lynch mobs, even if their noose is only rhetorical. We need more peacemakers. It's the peacemakers who save the world from the unthinking mob.

My father was a peacemaker. He believed in civil discourse. He believed in respectful dialogue. He believed that sometimes compromise for the sake of finding common ground is a noble and courageous act. From him I learned that to be a peacemaker often involves dissenting from the majority, especially from the "crowd," and most of all from the angry crowd. The angry crowd wants only to assert its will, and this is often done in the destructive form of revenge and scapegoating. The angry crowd is cruel, stupid, and dangerous. The peacemaker stands against the crowd. The peacemaker is the one who tries to create space for mercy and truth. Sadly, this is why so many of the great peacemakers of history have ended up as martyrs—from Jesus to Gandhi to Martin Luther King Jr.

Søren Kierkegaard was saying the same thing my father taught me when he made this succinct observation: "The crowd *is* untruth." Kierkegaard then goes on to further indict the crowd with this stinging critique, "The crowd is indeed untruth. Christ was crucified because he would have nothing to do with the crowd."[1] Kierkegaard is right, and it's an important insight—Christ was almost always against the crowd. Consider these examples: When the crowd wanted to take Jesus by force and make him King, he hid from the crowd (John 6:15); when the crowd followed Jesus after he had fed the five thousand, Jesus intentionally offended the crowd to the extent that they all left him (John 6:22–59); when the crowd shouted for joy and acclaimed him King on Palm Sunday, Jesus wept because he knew the violent way of the crowd would lead to their eventual destruction (Luke 19:37–44); and when Jesus was in Jerusalem for the Feast of Tabernacles, we find this troubling exchange between Christ and the crowd: "Why are you looking for an opportunity to kill me?" The crowd answered, "You have a demon! Who is trying to kill you?" (John 7:19–20).

Of course the crowd *was* trying to kill Jesus, even if the crowd didn't know it yet. And it's deeply ironic that the crowd would raise the subject of demons. (As we shall see, crowd dynamics are closely associated with the demonic.) At the Feast of Tabernacles the crowd may have been unconscious to its homicidal intentions, but Jesus knew that revolutionary crowds advocating violence for their cause are driven by the demonic spirit of murder. Six months later, at the Feast of Passover, this same Jerusalem crowd would insist that Jesus be crucified. In a very real sense, we can attribute the death of Jesus to cowardly leaders capitulating to a crowd committed to violent action. Jesus knew why the crowd would seek to kill him—because he did not share their "truth" of killing in the name of "freedom." What we may venerate as freedom-loving revolutionaries, the cross exposes as a demonic mob quite capable of killing the innocent. We should never forget that Jesus was executed in the name of "freedom and justice"—whether it was the Roman version or the Jewish version. But the cross shames the ancient deception that freedom and justice can be attained by killing. The crowd believes this pernicious lie, but Christ never does. The Passover crowd shouted, "Hosanna!" ("Save now!") until it realized that Jesus wouldn't save them by killing their enemies; then it shouted, "Crucify him!" Jesus refused to be a messiah after the model of Alexander the Great, Julius Caesar, Judah Maccabeus, William Wallace, or George Washington—and the crowd despises him for it. The crowd loves their violent heroes. The crowd is predisposed to believe in the idea that "freedom and justice" can be achieved by violence. More on this later. What we need to recognize at this point is the dangerous nature of crowds.

A crowd under the influence of an angry, vengeful spirit is the most dangerous thing in the world. It is closely associated with the essence of what is satanic. The unholy spirit (think *mood* or *attitude*) of the satanic is the inclination to blame, accuse, and recriminate. (The words *satan* and *devil* both mean to accuse and blame.) When the satanic spirit of angry blame and accusation infects a crowd, a perilous phenomenon is born. The crowd abandons truth as it searches for a target upon which it can express the pent-up rage it feels. I say "it" because the angry crowd takes on a life of its own. The crowd is now in search of a scapegoat, whose role it is to bear the sin of the crowd. It works like this: When a group of people perceive themselves to be slighted or wronged, displaced or threatened, they can metastasize into a vindictive crowd. When a group of people becomes an angry, fear-driven crowd, the groupthink phenomenon of mob mentality quickly overtakes rational thought and individual responsibility. The mob takes on a spirit of its own and the satanic is generated. The mob becomes capable of evil that would be unthinkable for most people as an individual. It can be as spontaneous as the Rwandan genocide or as systematic as the Nazi's Final Solution. The vindictive crowd is now possessed by enormous negative energy. This negative energy has the potential to turn the crowd against itself. The crowd (though not necessarily its individual members) seems to know this. An outlet for the crowd's anger must be found. The crowd has the demonic instinct to select a scapegoat—a sacrificial victim to bear the sinful anger of the crowd. As soon as the scapegoat is identified, the crowd proceeds to blame, shame, accuse, vilify, and possibly murder the scapegoat.

The scapegoat is usually a marginalized person or a minority group that is easy to victimize. But the crowd does not admit that it has selected a weak victim as a scapegoat. The crowd must continue to practice the self-deception that the scapegoat is a real threat to "freedom" or "righteousness" or whatever the crowd is using to justify its fear-based insecurity and anger. This is why foreigners, immigrants, racial minorities, and religious minorities are often selected as scapegoats. Jews have had a long, tragic history of being victimized as scapegoats. As the destructive energy of the demonized crowd is released upon the scapegoat victim, a kind of "miracle" occurs—peace is restored and unity is achieved within the crowd. Simply put, the crowd "feels better." The crowd has been saved from its own demonic anger. This "escape valve" of sacrificing a scapegoat is highly effective in producing a sense of well-being and belonging within the crowd. Human beings have been utilizing the "scapegoat mechanism," as René Girard calls it, since the dawn of human civilization. It's the blood-drenched altar of civilization. It's the Cain model for preserving the polis. It's collective murder as the alchemy for peace and unity. The crowd vents its violence and vengeance upon a scapegoat to protect itself *from itself*. But this dark secret is hidden from the crowd. The crowd believes the satanic lie that the scapegoat has to be vilified and sacrificed for the sake of "truth" or "freedom" or some other noble but ill-defined ideal. What's undeniable is that the scapegoat mechanism does produce a peace and unity among the dominant majority. It's also demonic. It's evil. As my dad taught me long ago—the majority is almost always wrong.

This is why if you follow an angry crowd—even if it calls itself Christian—you are likely to be wrong. Even if you're not wrong in the actual *issue*, you will probably be wrong in *spirit*. So never follow an angry crowd. Never! An angry person is bad enough, but an angry crowd is diabolical! Without any hyperbole, I insist that a crowd under the sway of an angry spirit is the most dangerous thing in the world. Massacres, slaughters, crusades, pogroms, genocides, and the Holocaust are what can happen when people follow an angry crowd in search of a scapegoat. Let us be clear on this: Jesus does *not* lead his people as an angry crowd. Jesus does *not* lead his people to join an angry crowd. Jesus never leads anything other than a gentle and peaceable minority. Jesus hides from the triumphalistic crowd that tries to force him to be their war-waging king. Jesus weeps over the nationalistic crowd whose hosannas are meant to egg him into violent revolution. The crowd is antichrist.

The angry crowd, in its cruel sacrifice of a scapegoat, is the opposite of Jesus's teaching of cosuffering love for neighbor and enemy. The crowd, with its shared fantasies of imagined enemies, is an exercise in unholy unity. But here is why it's such a powerful deception: it doesn't *feel* unholy. It feels holy; it feels spiritual; it feels patriotic; it feels right. It has a deeply religious aura to it. It *is* a spiritual experience. The spiritual experience of expressing a shared hostility can even be confused for the Holy Spirit ... because of how it *feels*. It's what's so seductive and dangerous about religious rants against popular scapegoats: liberals, socialists, gays, Muslims, immigrants, etc. A unity *is* achieved around this kind of angry rhetoric, a unity that is undeniably cathartic and religious. But it is cathartic and religious in the wrong way. As Kierkegaard said, "To win a crowd is no art; for that only untruth is needed, nonsense, and a little knowledge of human passions."[2]

To follow Christ is to differ from the crowd. To differ from the crowd is to be controversial. To be controversial by differing from the crowd is to run the risk of becoming a scapegoat yourself. And this is exactly what Jesus became—the innocent scapegoat who ended the injustice of scapegoating. Jesus became the sacrificial victim who ended violent sacrifice. In dying at the hands of our sins, Jesus saved us from scapegoating and violent sacrifice. Jesus will never lead a crowd. Jesus will only lead his little flock: "Do not be afraid little flock, for it is your Father's good pleasure to give you the kingdom"—Jesus (Luke 12:32).

Jesus's flock is never a crowd; it's always a "little" flock—no matter how numerous his followers. Even if the flock of baptized Christ followers in the world today numbers two billion, it is still Jesus's little flock. We cannot turn Jesus's little flock into the crowd. When the little flock becomes an angry crowd, it has become antichrist and has ceased to follow the Good Shepherd. We have to choose between Christ and the crowd. Let me put it to you like this: Jesus loves you, but he may not love the crowd you have aligned yourself with. To follow Jesus requires the courage to leave the crowd and join his little flock, one not driven by the demonic spirit of fear. The little flock has heard its Shepherd say, "Do not be afraid." Because the little flock is not driven by fear, it does not become an angry crowd or need to form an angry "us" movement in opposition to an imagined enemy "them." The little flock receives the kingdom as a gift flowing from the sheer good pleasure of God. Once we realize God's government is given as a gift, we never again need to fight, harm, or kill for any other government.

To follow Jesus and his little flock instead of following the demonized crowd, it is important to see scapegoating for the deep evil that it is. Scapegoating is all around us, but it can be hard to perceive. To understand how the scapegoat mechanism works, it may be helpful to think about the dynamics of the childhood playground. (This is a theme explored by Nobel laureate, William Golding, in his 1954 novel, *Lord of the Flies*.) Like most people, my first encounter with the dark world of scapegoating was on the playground in elementary school. I can see that now. But as I attempt to describe the scapegoat mechanism, bear in mind this phenomenon occurs *unconsciously*—for they know not what they do. "To have a scapegoat is not to know that one has one. As soon as the scapegoat is revealed and named as such, it loses its power."[3] Scapegoating is done instinctively but not innocently. It *is* sinful. Here's how scapegoating happens at the adolescent playground level. Boys at play (and girls in their own way) generate a lot of competition—who's the strongest; who's the fastest; who's the toughest? The awareness of competition creates a certain amount of tension and anxiety among the children, but the playground crowd knows what to do with it. A scapegoat is chosen. Usually someone who is different, weaker, or less able to retaliate. Maybe the overweight kid, the weak kid, the "sissy" kid, the kid without friends. This unfortunate child becomes the target, the victim, the sacrifice, the scapegoat. The selected scapegoat is mocked, ridiculed, and picked on. He's chosen for this abuse because the crowd has unconsciously agreed that he will be the target of their anxiety. He is innocent, but he becomes the sacrifice. The danger the playground crowd poses to *itself* is channeled on to a single victim—the scapegoat. As the gang of boys releases its competitive anxiety on to the unfortunate scapegoat, there is a palpable sense of relief. Peace is restored to the playground. The members of the gang are relieved that "it's not *me* being picked on, because it's *him*"—the fat kid, the skinny kid, the weak kid, the ugly kid, the new kid, the different kid. The playground is now safe … except for the scapegoat.

Again, I'm not suggesting that a group of ten-year-old boys does this *consciously*. (Or even adults, for that matter.) Of course we don't do it consciously, but we do it. We do it through an inherited dark instinct. I can rummage through my memories and recall this kind of scapegoat mechanism being employed in my childhood years. And I'm saddened by it. Even these many years later I can remember the names of those most often selected to be the scapegoat. Through no fault of their own, they were forced to bear the insecurities—the "sins," if you will—of the rest. It may seem like nothing more than "kids being kids," but it's not innocent. It is, in fact, an adolescent inauguration into the demonic. The fear of being exposed ... the group selection of the one to be picked on ... the relief that it's not you ... the bonding achieved by the crowd's cruelty to the scapegoat. ... All of this is what the satanic is about. It's also what human sacrifice is about. Unfortunately, as we leave the playground for adulthood, we don't leave scapegoating behind; we just become more sophisticated with it. But scapegoating is one of the evils Jesus came to save the world from. He did it by becoming the ultimate scapegoat—by dying for our sins.

The word *scapegoat* has its origins in the Bible. In Leviticus chapter 16, the King James Version of the Bible translates the Hebrew word *azazel* as "scapegoat." The *azazel* was the banished goat that carried the sins of Israel into the wilderness. In other words, an innocent animal was blamed and banished and in this manner bore the sins of Israel. (Which was a vast improvement over human sacrifice!) Over time, *scapegoat* came to mean a person blamed by the crowd for the wrongdoing of others. But we must face the truth that scapegoating, though effective in producing peace and unity in the community, is a sin to be saved from. What is sinful about it is that an innocent person (or minority group) suffers for the sins of the crowd. It is untruth. It is injustice.

The gospel narratives make it clear that Jesus filled the role of scapegoat. With his crucifixion Jesus defused the powder keg of tension that had been building in Jerusalem during the governorship of Pontius Pilate. Jesus was a scapegoat for Pilate and Caiaphas and for the dangerous crowds they both sought to appease. We even have the curious remark about how the Roman governor Pontius Pilate and the Jewish king Herod Agrippa became friends around their mockery and condemnation of Jesus.

> Even Herod with his soldiers treated him with contempt and mocked him; then he put an elegant robe on him, and sent him back to Pilate. That same day Herod and Pilate became friends; before this they had been enemies. (Luke 23:11–12)

Do you see how it works? These two powerful adversaries—Pilate and Herod—found a way to neutralize their enmity and become friends. They did it by treating Jesus with cruelty and contempt, by making him an object of mockery. Pilate and Herod found a scapegoat for their fear and loathing. Through the "miracle" of the scapegoat, these two dangerous rivals relaxed and became friends. Just like on the playground. Except that instead of taunts, their cruelty took the form of torture and crucifixion. Instead of a nameless, helpless victim to play the role of the scapegoat, they picked on the Son of God. *And that's the point!* By becoming a scapegoat, Jesus dragged the demonic practice of scapegoating into the light where it could be named, shamed, and once and for all rejected!

On the cross Jesus took the blame. All the blame. Our sinful addiction to blaming others—Jesus took that upon himself. He was innocent, but he took the blame anyway. Caiaphas blamed Jesus; Pilate blamed Jesus; Herod blamed Jesus; the crowd blamed Jesus—and Jesus took the blame. The practice of blaming is given a place to die in Jesus. Jesus carried our blame down to Hades—where it belongs—and left it there. Jesus became the final scapegoat. The innocent one, suffering, praying from the cross, "Father, forgive them, for they know not what they do" (Luke 23:34 ESV). And Jesus was telling the truth from the cross—we do not know what we are doing when we blame the scapegoat. We have been deceived by the crowd, by the satan, by the spirit of fear. So Jesus died for our sins. Jesus died at the hands of humans under the satanic impulse to blame. Jesus died as an innocent victim of the demonic scapegoat system that the crowd always resorts to. And he died with forgiveness on his lips. Jesus took the blame to do away with blaming. Jesus bore the accusation to do away with accusing. Jesus became the scapegoat banished to the wilderness of death. But then something new happened.

The banished scapegoat came back! Three days later Jesus was vindicated by God the Father in resurrection! But in his return from the wilderness of death, Jesus did not speak of revenge; instead he spoke of peace and forgiveness. (See John 20:19–23.) Yes, Jesus forgives us, but he also calls us to forsake the evil practice of turning people into scapegoats. Jesus says to a humanity that has built its civilizations upon the blood of sacrificial victims, "I forgive you, but we're not going to play this way anymore." No more cruelty. No more blame. No more scapegoating. No more sacrificing. No more trying to shape the world by the violent sacrifice of collective murder. Jesus is the Lamb of God who ends sacrifice!

Do you remember what Jesus said about sacrifice? "Go and learn what this means, 'I desire mercy, not sacrifice'" (Matt. 9:13 NIV). Mercy and *not* sacrifice! Jesus also said something else about sacrifice: "If you had known what these words mean, 'I desire mercy, not sacrifice,' you would not have condemned the innocent" (Matt. 12:7 NIV). Of course Jesus was the innocent one condemned to be a sacrifice. But Jesus is to be the last innocent victim condemned to suffer as a scapegoat for the sake of an angry crowd. The cross is to transform us. When we look at what scapegoating did to Jesus, we repent of it. His innocent death shocks us into realizing we cannot participate in a system that can do *that* to a sinless man. If scapegoating is responsible for the greatest crime of all—the murder of God!—we must once and for all abandon our demonic practice of blame shifting. It was human systems of blame, sacrifice, and violence that put the Son of God to death. But this sacrificial death drags the sin of the world into the light where it is forgiven by Christ and where it is to be forsaken by us. "Jesus, of all the victims who have ever been, is the only one capable of revealing the true nature of violence."[4] Jesus forgives us. Jesus understands that we "know not what we do." That we are caught in an evil system of achieving peace through violence. But now we must rethink our lives and resolve to live according to Jesus's alternative way of producing peace. The Jesus way of producing peace is based in mercy and forgiveness, not blame and retribution. We must not continue to build Babylon upon the blood of sacrificial victims—instead we are invited to join the New Jerusalem built on the blood of Jesus. Jesus is the Lamb of God who became the final scapegoat. Jesus is the sacrificial victim who shows us that sacrifice is not what God wants. God wants mercy, not sacrifice; forgiveness, not scapegoating. Jesus is the Good Shepherd who forgives us and calls us out of the crowd and into his little flock.

So what do we do with this? How do we go about renouncing the sinful system of projecting blame onto a scapegoat? We might start by turning off the radio when the manipulative talk-show host tries to agitate the listening crowd into the evil of scapegoating. We might refuse to follow religious leaders who gain a following by the rhetorical lynching of the usual scapegoats. We might decide to stop practicing in our adult lives the juvenile playground politics of scapegoating the easy targets. We might tattoo our mind with these three transformational truths:

> The majority is almost always wrong.
> The crowd is untruth.
> Scapegoating is demonic.

All of this means that the little flock of Jesus need no longer traffic in the stock and trade finger-pointing and scapegoating of power-obsessed politics. We don't belong to the fear-based crowd desperate to control others through political power. We've been liberated from that worn-out paradigm. We don't need to manage our fear like that anymore. We've heard Jesus tell us not to be afraid because it's the Father's good pleasure to give us the kingdom. Receiving God's government as a sheer gift of grace liberates us from the anxious drive to fight for "our rights." Because we pray, "Thy kingdom come," we don't have to desperately clutch to some mythical past. We can believe in the future. Dread gives way to hope.

Because God loves us, we don't have to be afraid. Because God loves us, we are free to love others—even our enemies. And after all, once you take fear off the table, how many enemies do you really have? We don't need to blame. We don't need to multiply enemies. We don't need to react to our fear by blaming a scapegoat. Only the fearful who don't know they are loved by God need to sacrifice scapegoats. God doesn't want that. He never did. God wants mercy. He always did. We didn't always know this, but now we do. Peace is no longer to be achieved by the illegitimate means of sacrificing a scapegoat. Peace is now given to us freely by the crucified and risen scapegoat. Fear has no place in the new world that Jesus inaugurates in his resurrection. We're called to be peacemakers, and peacemakers cannot be fearmongers. The biggest difference between a peacemaker and a fearmonger is whether or not they really believe in the unconditional love of God. As ecumenical Patriarch Bartholomew has said:

> Unless our actions are founded on love, rather than on fear, they will never be able to overcome fanaticism or fundamentalism. ... Only those who know—deep inside the heart—that they are loved can be true peacemakers. Our peacemaking ultimately stems from and relates to love for all of God's creation, both human and environmental.
>
> In this form, peacemaking is a radical response to policies of violence and the politics of power.[5]

The crowd sustains itself by sacrificing a scapegoat—by finding someone or some group to blame. The crowd exists by the untruth that the world is a closed system where there's never enough. The crowd is a coalition of fear. The crowd is a coward with a gun.

But Jesus's little flock is not like the crowd. They have no need for a scapegoat. They know Jesus has already taken all the blame. The little flock knows that this world is not a closed system; it is a world open to the infinite grace of God. The little flock is not afraid, because it is formed around the Perfect Love that drives out all fear. They know that the majority is almost always wrong, but they love them anyway, and they seek to draw the crowd out of their fear and into a liberated world sustained by the love of God.

Christ is against the crowd because of the crowd's deep inhumanity and dark allegiance with the satan. But Christ calls to each soul lost in the crowd, seeking to gather all of us to his little flock—a flock redeemed from the demonic crowd learning to live beyond fear and without a need for scapegoats. The flock liberated from fear, living together peaceably, never building unity on a sacrificial "them"—this is the universal flock of the Prince of Peace. That the world might become the little flock of Christ is the peacemaker's hopeful dream.

CHAPTER 4

IT'S HARD TO
BELIEVE IN JESUS

How can we forget the morning of September 11, 2001? We remember a beautiful dawn and azure skies. We remember the strangeness of the empty skies in the days that followed. We can tell our story of where we were and how we heard about what has come to be known simply as 9/11.

Like all of us, I remember that day. I remember church staff gathering around a television with transfixed stares. I remember the sheer incredulity when the towers fell. I remember meeting with a group of pastors that day to hastily organize a citywide prayer service. I remember how thousands came to this gathering. I remember the prayer I prayed …

And I'm ashamed of it.

If I could, I would take back the prayer I prayed on that terrible day.

The terrorist attack of 9/11 was a horrific crime. A national tragedy. It was a visitation of demonic evil. It brought the appalling loss of three thousand lives. It brought a sickening end to a short-lived optimism. When the Berlin Wall came down, a new optimism was born. Twelve years later the Twin Towers came down, and that optimism died. September 11, 2001, was the Pearl Harbor for a new generation of Americans. We now fear 9/11 was an ominous harbinger for the new century.

But 9/11 was also a test. It was a test for America in ways that we are still coming to terms with. It's a test for our democracy as we struggle to balance security and liberty. In different ways 9/11 was a test for the American church. Will we succumb to the temptation of scapegoating? Will the church scapegoat Muslims in the twenty-first century as the church scapegoated Jews in previous centuries? For me it was a personal test of my commitment to the Jesus way of responding to violence and enemies. I failed the test. Miserably. My failure came in the form of a prayer. Allow me to tell my story.

On the night of 9/11, as our nation reeled from the shock that day, I stood on a platform in the gymnasium at Missouri Western State University. I was there as a pastor. My pastoral vocation is to guide people in following the Jesus way. My task that night was to pray—to lead our city in a prayerful response to the traumatic events of 9/11. On that strange and confusing night, I failed in my role as a Christian pastor. I prayed a prayer based on anger and vengeance. I prayed a prayer to sanction US military retaliation. I prayed a war prayer. Oh, I'm sure I prayed in appropriate ways as well—for the rescue workers, for the missing, for their families, for comfort from above, etc. But for the most part, my prayer was a petition for God to take our side in the inevitable war to come. Yes, it was a war prayer. And I could *feel* how my prayer energized the crowd. The *crowd* certainly did not think I had failed. The crowd thought I had passionately expressed to God the very thing they were feeling. Many in the crowd would have described my prayer as "anointed." I don't presume every person present shared that sentiment, but there is no doubt that the *crowd* was with me. The crowd wanted a war prayer, and that's what I prayed. I gave the crowd what it wanted. I wish I had done better. I wish my prayer had been more of a broken lament. I wish my prayer had been a tearful cry for mercy. I wish my prayer had been an honest wrestling with Jesus's call to love our enemies ... even if it had only been to express how impossible it seemed at that moment. But I didn't do those things. I prayed a war prayer. At that time I didn't know about Mark Twain's *War Prayer*. I wish I had.

Around 1904, probably in reflection upon the Philippine-American War, Mark Twain wrote a short story entitled *The War Prayer*. Twain begins his story by telling us, "The country was up in arms, the war was on, in every breast burned the holy fire of patriotism."[1] Twain paints the picture of the sudden appearance of flags, patriotic oratory, and military parades. (Remember the flags and patriotism following 9/11?) But at the center of the story is a scathing critique of the Christian response to a popular war. Twain writes, "In the churches the pastors preached devotion to flag and country and invoked the God of Battles beseeching His aid in our good cause."[2] I remember how we hung a giant American flag on the side of our church following 9/11. People loved it. And we remember how the churches were full following 9/11. In Twain's story, on the Sunday following the declaration of war, a pastor ascended to his pulpit in a packed church and prayed a long and passionate prayer for God's blessing upon the coming conflict. Twain gives the reader a summary of the pastor's eloquent war prayer:

> The burden of its supplication was that an ever-merciful and benignant Father of us all would watch over our noble young soldiers, and aid, comfort, and encourage them in their patriotic work; bless them, shield them in the day of battle and the hour of peril, bear them in His mighty hand, make them strong and confident, invincible in the bloody onset; help them crush the foe, grant to them and to their flag and country imperishable honor and glory.[3]

Such prayers are familiar enough. They are based on the assumption that war is the only conceivable course of action and that if we will but ask, God himself will bless our martial endeavors. But at the close of the pastor's prayer, Twain tells how an "aged stranger" entered the church, moved to the pulpit, and announced to the congregation that he had been sent by God to interpret the prayer the pastor had prayed and to which the congregation had given hearty assent. The stranger instructed the congregation that their prayer was *really* this:

> O Lord our Father, our young patriots, idols of our hearts, go forth into battle—be Thou near them! With them—in spirit—we also go forth from the sweet peace of our beloved firesides to smite the

foe. O Lord our God, help us tear their soldiers to bloody shreds with our shells; help us to cover their smiling fields with the pale forms of their patriot dead; help us to drown the thunder of the guns with the shrieks of their wounded, writhing in pain; help us to lay waste their humble homes with a hurricane of fire; help us to wring the hearts of their unoffending widows with unavailing grief; help us to turn them out roofless with their little children to wander unfriended the wastes of their desolated land in rags and hunger and thirst, sports of the sun flames of summer and the icy winds of winter, broken in spirit, worn with travail, imploring Thee for the refuge of the grave and denied it—for our sakes who adore Thee, Lord, blast their hopes, blight their lives, protract their bitter pilgrimage, make heavy their steps, water their way with their tears, stain the white snow with the blood of their wounded feet! We ask it, in the spirit of love, of Him Who is the Source of Love, and Who is the ever-faithful refuge and friend of all that are sore beset and seek His aid with humble and contrite hearts. Amen.[4]

After a pause, the mysterious stranger said, "Ye have prayed it; if ye still desire it, speak!" Twain ends his short story with this pessimistic sentence: "It was believed afterward that the man was a lunatic, because there was no sense in what he said."[5]

I share Twain's indicting story because I am a pastor who has prayed a war prayer. It wasn't as egregious as the one in Twain's story, but it was a war prayer nevertheless. I wish I had done better on my 9/11 test, and I believe today I would, but on that day I failed. All I can do about my past failure is ask for forgiveness—forgiveness from God and from those I poorly led. I have asked and received forgiveness from both. The other thing I can do is resolve that I will never make the same mistake again.

In Twain's story the congregation concluded that the mysterious stranger was mad. But it wasn't the stranger who was mad. The stranger spoke the sanity of heaven. The stranger simply removed the religious veneer from the war prayer. No, the stranger was not mad; it is *we* who are mad. We are mad if we imagine that the God of love revealed in Jesus will bless us in waging war. *That* is madness! But it's a pervasive and beloved madness. And I know from experience that it's hard to oppose a crowd fuming for war. When we have identified a hated enemy, we want to be assured that God is on our side as we go to war with our enemy. And we believe that surely God *is* on our side, because we *feel* so unified in the moment. Everyone knows the nation is most unified in times of war. Nothing unites a nation like war. But what's so tragic is when Christian leaders pretend that a rally around the war god is compatible with worshipping the God revealed in Jesus Christ. We refuse to face the truth that waging war is incompatible with following Jesus. We forget that God is most clearly revealed, not in the nascent understanding of the ancient Hebrews but in the Word made flesh. We forget that "being disguised under the disfigurement of an ugly crucifixion and death, the Christform upon the cross is paradoxically the clearest revelation of who God is."[6] We forget that "the worst day in history was not a Tuesday in New York, but a Friday in Jerusalem when a consortium of clergy and politicians colluded to run the world on our own terms by crucifying God's own Son."[7] We forget that when we see Christ dead upon the cross, we discover a God who would rather die than kill his enemies. We forget all of this because the disturbing truth is this—it's hard to believe in Jesus.

When I say it's hard to believe in Jesus, I mean it's hard to believe in Jesus's *ideas*—in his way of saving the world. For Christians it's not hard to believe in Jesus as the Son of God, the Second Person of the Trinity—all the Christological stuff the church hammered out in the first five centuries. That's not hard for us. What's hard is to believe in Jesus as a political theologian. It's hard because his ideas for running the world are so radically different from anything we are accustomed to. Which is why, I suspect, for so long, the Gospels have been treated as mere narratives and have not been taken seriously as theological documents in their own right. We want to hear how Jesus was born in Bethlehem, died on the cross, and rose again on the third day. We use these historical bits as the raw material for our theology that we mostly shape from a particular misreading of Paul. In doing this we conveniently screen out Jesus's own teachings about the kingdom of God and especially his ideas about nonviolence and enemy love.

In recent years I have participated in a number of public discussions about the Sermon on the Mount. These discussions inevitably end up focusing on Jesus's revolutionary ideas about nonviolent resistance of evil and loving our enemies.

> You have heard that it was said, "An eye for an eye
> and a tooth for a tooth." But I say to you, Do not
> resist an evildoer. But if anyone strikes you on the
> right cheek, turn the other also. (Matt 5:38–39)

> You have heard that it was said, "You shall love your
> neighbor and hate your enemy." But I say to you,
> Love your enemies and pray for those who perse-
> cute you. (Matt. 5:43–44)

What always happens in these discussions (every time!) is that there are those who feel uneasy with the implications of Jesus's teaching on nonviolence and enemy love. They instinctively know that taken seriously, these radical political ideas place a lot of pressure on existing political and social structures. Reacting to their unease, they begin to explain what Jesus did *not* mean by "resist not an evildoer" and when this teaching does *not* apply. (By the way, Hitler *always* shows up in these discussions.) Creating exemptions for the Sermon on the Mount and explaining when and where Jesus's teaching does not apply is fine (in theory, I suppose); but at some point you have to decide what Jesus *did* mean with his kingdom imperatives on nonviolence and enemy love. Which is to say, we eventually have to ask ourselves what *did* Jesus intend and when *do* we need to turn the other cheek? If our default response to this portion of the Sermon on the Mount is to craft exemptions, we might give the impression that we really don't believe in Jesus's ideas of nonviolent resistance and enemy love *at all*. Which is what I mean when I say it's hard to believe in Jesus. It's just plain difficult to believe in Jesus and remain comfortable with the ancient assumption that violence and war are legitimate ways of shaping the world and achieving justice. But we *are* comfortable with the ancient assumption, and it *is* hard to believe in Jesus. This is what the apostle John seems to be getting at when he tells us something significant about Jesus's complicated relationship with his family: "Not even his brothers believed in him" (John 7:5).

Jesus own brothers didn't believe in him! What does that mean? Of course we are not to view the disbelief of Jesus's brothers in an anachronistic way, thinking it means they did not believe their brother was the Second Person of the Trinity (as if they were heretics at the Council of Nicaea). Jesus's brothers would indeed come to believe that their elder brother was divine but only after the resurrection. At this point the issue at hand was whether or not Jesus was the Messiah—the true King of the Jews who would rescue Israel. *What Jesus's brothers didn't believe was that Jesus could be the Messiah by going about it the way he was!* Everyone knew that if you were going to be the Messiah and rescue Israel, you would have to be like Joshua, like David, like Judah Maccabaeus. These Jewish war heroes provided the prototype for the Messiah. The Messiah was to be a conqueror like Joshua, a warrior like David, an avenger like Judah Maccabaeus. But Jesus kept talking about forgiveness, loving enemies, turning the other cheek. Who could believe in a nonviolent Messiah? A nonviolent Messiah was incongruent. John wants us to know that not even Jesus's own brothers could believe in a Messiah like that!

Jesus's brothers didn't believe Jesus could be Messiah *and* live what he was preaching. They were incompatible agendas. Jesus could be a rabbi teaching nonviolence and enemy love *or* he could be the

Messiah who would save Israel—but not both. The miracles Jesus was performing spoke for themselves. It was obvious that God was with Jesus. But if he were to fulfill his Messianic mission and liberate Israel, he would have to depart from what he was teaching in the Sermon on the Mount. It was in this sense that Jesus's brothers did not believe him. Which is basically the same sense in which we—the modern-day brothers of Jesus—do not believe in him. We believe in Jesus theologically, religiously, spiritually, sentimentally … but not politically. We believe Jesus is the Second Person of the Trinity, but we don't really believe he was a competent political theologian. If we were tasked with framing a political theology drawn only from Jesus's words, what would it look like? It would probably look like something we don't much believe in. Why? Because when it comes to political models for running the world, we find it hard to believe in Jesus.

Jesus's response to his brothers' disbelief is enormously significant. When he realized that even his own brothers did not believe he could be the Messiah if he refused to take up the sword, Jesus said, "The world cannot hate you, but it hates me because I testify against it that its works are evil" (John 7:7).

We need to be careful not to rush past this. It's all too easy to hear this simple sentence as religious jargon and move on without a moment's thought. Let's not do that. What was Jesus really saying here? Jesus was telling his brothers (James, Joses, Judas, and Simon according to Mark 6:3) that the world hated *him* but not *them*. What are we to make of this? Why did Jesus say the world hated him but not his brothers? Jesus said it's because he testified against the evil deeds of the world and he testified against the world *in a way that his brothers did not.* But what evil of the world is Jesus talking about? Surely Jesus's brothers "called sin, sin," as we say. Or are we to imagine that Jesus's brother known in the church as James the Just, famous for his piety, was not opposed to immorality, drunkenness, debauchery, and the like? (Which is the kind of evil we tend to think of as "the world.") Are we to picture James as a profligate sinner unwilling to testify against conventional sin? Of course not. James and the rest of Jesus's brothers were observant and pious Jews, and as such they would have condemned immorality and impiety. So what evil *did* Jesus testify against that his brothers did *not*? What was this evil that the world, including Jesus's brothers, was comfortable with, but which Jesus testified against? What evil of the world did Jesus expose and, in so doing, cause the world to hate him—even to the extent of seeking to kill him? It was the systemic and hidden evil that is *the very foundation of the world!*

As the climax of the Hebrew prophetic tradition, Jesus did not merely testify against symptomatic sin—in fact, he spent very little time doing this. Rather, Jesus struck at the heart of the systemic evil that has provided the foundation for human civilization. Jesus didn't seem very interested in exposing symptomatic sinners—tax collectors, drunkards, prostitutes, etc. Instead Jesus challenged the guardians of systemic sin—the power brokers of religion and politics. Jesus knew that tax collectors were greedy and violent, but he was more interested in focusing his prophetic critique on the foundations of greed and violence that inevitably produce greedy and violent people. Sinful tax collectors were merely a symptom of a sinful *but hidden* system. The sinful and hidden system of greed and violence is "the world." Jesus, in his prophetic preaching, was shining a light on the dark foundation of the world: "I will open my mouth to speak in parables; I will proclaim what has been hidden from the foundation of the world" (Matt. 13:35).

Jesus testified against the systemic sin that had organized the world since Cain killed his brother and founded human civilization. From Cain onward, a world defined by war organized itself around groupthink hostility and sanctioned the violence that flows from it. Whether it was agriculturists against nomads, Egyptians against Kushites, Babylonians against Hittites, Greeks against Persians, Trojans again Spartans, Jews against Romans—the world had been arranged around shared hatred and collective murder.

Look at the borders on a map. What are they? Nearly always they are the boundaries of ancient enmities where the blood of hated victims has been shed. Lines on a map, far from being benign, tell a bloody tale. At the dawn of human civilization, tribal identities were formed around a shared hostility toward an enemy "them." Contrary to what Rousseau romantically imaged, anthropologists insist there was never a time when human communities lived peaceably and without war. The shared identity necessary for organizing the world was based around a common hatred—a common hatred hallowed in collective murder.

The relentless bloodletting of Homer's Iliad depicts the foundational evil of the world that Jesus dared to testify against. Homer's epic poem recounting the Trojan War became a sacred text within the pagan world consistent with the world's bloody foundation. The blind bard saw more than most and knew what made the world go around—rage and murder. The Spartans needed to hate and scapegoat the Trojans so they could achieve a unity within their own

society. They needed to project the anxiety that threatened to erupt
into an every-man-for-himself violence onto a sacrificial "them"—an
enemy whom they could hate in common and kill with impunity.
They needed to kill, but they also needed to believe that killing was
good. This is the basic (though hidden) political foundation of the
world. It's also evil. It's an evil so well hidden that we hardly ever see
it as evil. It's an evil concealed behind flags, anthems, monuments,
memorials, and the rhetoric of those who have won their wars. The
hidden foundation of hatred and murder is why world history is
little more than the record of who killed who, where, when, and
what for.

In a study of world history, you will meet far more warriors
than poets; far more generals than artists. Jesus testified against this
violent arrangement of the world. Jesus wanted to show us that the
"heroic" murder of our enemy brothers is, in truth, evil. But we
don't see it as evil. We see it as simply the only way things can be.
We see it as the bedrock foundation of the world. It's almost impossible for us to see it as evil. Not even Jesus's brothers could see the
world as evil in the way Jesus did.

So when Jesus comes along and says to us, "Love your enemy,"
we instinctively feel how radical it is. He's not just giving individuals a personal ethic; he is striking at the very foundation of the
world! The world was founded on hating enemies, and now Jesus
says, "Don't do it!" When Jesus said, "Turn the other cheek," he
wasn't just trying to produce kinder, gentler people; he was trying
to refound the world! Instead of retaliatory violence; the world is to
be refounded on cosuffering love. Jesus understood that the world
had built its societal structures upon shared hatred, scapegoating,

and what René Girard calls "sacred violence." In challenging "sacred violence" (which Israel cherished in their war stories), Jesus was challenging the world at its most basic level. We cherish, honor, and salute sacred violence. We have to! We have a dark instinct that we must honor Cain's war against Abel—and our own wars upon our hated enemies—or our whole system will fall apart. But Jesus testified against it—that those deeds were evil.

This is where the tension begins to build. What Jesus called evil are the very things our cultures and societies have honored in countless myths, memorials, and anthems. It was this deep insight into the dark foundations of the world that Jesus possessed and his brothers did not. James and the rest of Jesus's brothers and disciples could testify against symptomatic evil of greed and immorality, but they could not testify against the systemic evil of hating national enemies. This is why the world hates Jesus in a way it could not hate his brothers. Ultimately, Jesus's brothers belonged to the same system as Caesar, Herod, and Caiaphas—the system of hating and seeking to kill one's national or ethnic enemy.

Jesus's call to love our enemies presents us with a problem—a problem that goes well beyond the challenge we find in trying to live out an ethic of enemy love on a personal level. How can a nation exist without hating its enemies? If nations can't hate and scapegoat their enemies, how can they cohere? If societies can't project blame onto a hated "other," how can they keep from turning on themselves? Jesus's answer is as simple as it is revolutionary: instead of an arrangement around hate and violence, the world is now to be arranged around love and forgiveness. The fear of our enemy and the pain of being wronged is not to be transferred through blame but dispelled through forgiveness. Unity is not to be built around the practice of scapegoating a hated victim but around the practice of loving your neighbor as yourself—even if your neighbor is your enemy. Jesus was trying to lead humanity into the deep truth that there is no "them;" there is only us.

Of course the principalities and powers of the old order (political and religious) hate this. The bloody world bequeathed by Cain hates anyone who testifies that its system of enmity and sacred violence is evil. This is why Jesus knew the world would hate him. He would try to teach the world the way of love that could lead us out of darkness, but not even his own brothers believed in what he was trying to do. So Jesus would have to go to the cross and allow himself to be murdered by the world—the system of hatred, scapegoating, and violence—so that it might be exposed for what it is. Pilate, Herod, and Caiaphas, as the political and religious representatives of the world's ancient system, acted accordingly and crucified Jesus Christ. Lost in the darkness of a system sustained by violence, they literally didn't know the terrible thing they were doing. With this in mind, we can hear in a fresh, new way what Jesus says from the cross: "Father, forgive them; for they do not know what they are doing" (Luke 23:34).

The cross is shock therapy for a world addicted to solving its problems through violence. The cross shocks us into the devastating realization that our system of violence murdered God! It was only after Jesus was raised from the dead that Jesus's brothers (or anyone) had the capacity to believe in Jesus in the fullest sense. Now that we know that "truly this was the Son of God," we look at the world in a new light. The things hidden from the foundation of the world have been revealed. The cross shames our ancient foundation. The cross strips naked the principalities and powers. The cross tears down the facade of glory that we use to hide the bodies of our slain victims.

In the light of the cross, we are to realize that if what we have built on Cain's foundation is capable of murdering the Son of God, the whole edifice needs to come down. In the light of the cross, our war anthems lose their luster. But this throws us into a crisis. What other alternatives are there? How else are we to arrange the world? The alternative is what Jesus is offering us when he told us that the kingdom of God is at hand. God's way of arranging the world around love and forgiveness is within reach. If we only dare to reach out for it, we can have it. But we are so afraid. We're not sure we can risk it. It's so hard for us to let go of the sword and take the hand of the crucified one. It's so hard for us to really believe in Jesus.

The crowd never believes in Jesus. Only the little flock that accepts its vulnerability can believe in Jesus. If you tell those rushing to war that their hatred of enemies and their plan for the organized killing of enemies is evil, the crowd will hate you. War is sacred. It lies beyond critique. To critique it is blasphemy. The crowd hates blasphemy. The crowd wants to kill blasphemers. The crowd knows that the criticism of their violence is blasphemy because they know their cause is just. They believe it. And from their perspective their cause *is* just. They can prove it. Both sides can prove it. Always. Achilles knew his cause was just and that it was perfectly legitimate to drag Hector's body from his chariot in front of the gates of Troy in a show of grotesque triumphalism. It's the same grotesque impulse that causes modern soldiers to pose for gruesome photos with the bodies of dead enemies. It's literally the way of the world.

But it's not the way of the new world founded by Jesus. Jesus is not the warrior king the world is accustomed to. Jesus is not the Jewish Achilles. Jesus refused to be the violent Messiah Israel longed for. Jesus did not kill Pilate and drag his body behind his chariot. Jesus did not pose triumphantly over the dead bodies of slain Roman soldiers. Instead it was Jesus who hung naked on a tree after being put to death through a state-sponsored execution. Jesus founded his kingdom in solidarity with brutalized victims. This is the gospel, but it's hard for us to believe in a Jesus who would rather die than kill his enemies. It's harder yet to believe in a Jesus who calls us to take up our own cross, follow him, and be willing to die rather than kill our enemies.

Many American Christians are fond of describing the United States as a "Christian nation"—which would mean a Christlike nation. With that in mind, here's a wild thought experiment. Imagine if Jesus went to Washington, DC. Imagine that he is invited to give a speech to a joint session of Congress. (He's Jesus after all, and I'm sure the senators and congressmen would be delighted to hear a speech from the founder of the world's largest religion—if nothing else it would confer great dignity upon their institution.) Imagine that the speech Jesus gave was his most famous sermon—the Sermon on the Mount. Can you imagine that?

Jesus is introduced. (Standing ovation.) He stands before Congress and begins to deliver his speech. "Blessed are the poor … the mourners … the meek." "Love your enemies." "Turn the other cheek." After a few perfunctory applauses early on, I'm pretty sure there would be a lot of squirming senators and uncomfortable congressmen. The room would sink into a tense silence. And when Jesus concluded his speech with a prophecy of the inevitable fall of the house that would not act upon his words (Matt. 7:26–27), what would Congress do? Nothing. They would not act. They could not act. To act on Jesus's words would undo their system. The Sermon on the Mount doesn't work in Cain's system—no matter how noble or sophisticated. In the end, the US Congress would no more adopt the policies Jesus set out in the Sermon on the Mount than they were adopted by the Jewish Sanhedrin or the Roman Senate.

The Jesus way and conventional power politics don't mix. So we tell Jesus to mind his own business—to go back to church and to "saving souls" and not to meddle in the real affairs of running the world. We sequester Jesus to a stained-glass quarantine and appropriate a trillion dollars for the war machine. This begs the question of why Christians get so worked up over which side has the most representatives in Congress when the entire system is incapable of implementing what Jesus taught. Do you see what I mean? It's *hard* to believe in Jesus! To believe in Jesus fully, to believe in Jesus as more than a personal Savior, to believe in Jesus without qualifications, to believe in Jesus as God's way to run the world, to believe in Jesus and his Sermon on the Mount, to believe in Jesus as the unimagined solution for a world gone wrong and *not* as merely chaplain or cheerleader for our favorite version of the status quo is very hard to do. It also very controversial.

If believing in Jesus were as easy as we pretend, it would have been easy for me to pass my 9/11 test. But it wasn't easy. And I didn't pass the test. I didn't wrestle with what Jesus calls his followers to do in the Sermon on the Mount. It didn't even cross my mind! I didn't pray about what it means to love my enemies. I prayed a war prayer.

I preached war sermons. Sermons like "The Road to Armageddon" and "Jesus, Jerusalem, and Jihad"—sermons in which I actually said, "We are at war with Islam." I'm ashamed of it now; I can barely stand to look at those sermon notes. But I preached those sermons. And they were popular sermons! People loved them. The crowd told me those sermons were anointed. When I was preaching my war sermons, I never once received any criticism for them. Never once! Telling the crowd that God is on our side is never a bad career move.

But a few years later, when I encountered Jesus in a fresh and new way, when I began to take the "words in red" seriously, when I repented for my war prayers and war sermons, when I started preaching peace sermons, then criticism came. Oh, believe me, it came! People left the church over my "new direction." My new direction was that I began to take the Sermon on the Mount seriously. My new direction was that I began to see the kingdom of Christ as God's alternative society. My new direction was to believe that peacemakers are the children of God. And I learned a bitter lesson. I learned that it is much easier to unite people around a Jesus who hates our enemies and blesses our wars than it is to unite people around a Jesus who calls us to love our enemies and pray for those who persecute us. It broke my heart to learn that people are not as easily drawn to a gospel of peace as they are to a rally for war. But I couldn't blame them. I had been the same way. I had endorsed war in the name of the Lord. I had prayed war prayers. I had preached war sermons. And if people became angry when I started praying peace prayers and preaching peace sermons, I couldn't be surprised. I had been the same way. Believing in a war-waging Messiah is easy. Believing in the Prince of Peace is hard.

CHAPTER 5

FREEDOM'S JUST
ANOTHER WORD FOR …

On Sunday, September 10, 2006, I was a guest speaker at a church in another state. It was the day before the fifth anniversary of 9/11. As part of the worship service, the church played a video with Lee Greenwood's patriotic anthem, "God Bless the USA," as the soundtrack. In part the lyrics say, "I'm proud to be an American where at least I know I'm free."

The video that accompanied this song consisted entirely of images of American military might—tanks, fighter jets, aircraft carriers, missiles being fired, soldiers with their weapons, and the like. During the familiar emotive chorus, the congregation began to sing along, with most lifting their hands in a posture of worship. I was dumbfounded. In a midwestern American church, Christians were worshipping before icons of war and singing a "hymn" about how proud they were to be Americans, to be "free." What was going on? Was this a mash-up of Mars and Jesus? It was weird. It was worship. It was wrong. And as far as I could tell, no one there sensed anything incongruent with replacing the cross with an M-1 tank and worshipping American military might while singing about a particular version of freedom. After the enthusiastic applause for "God Bless the USA," I was introduced and made my way to the pulpit. I lacked the courage to (or had the good sense not to) suggest to the congregation that what they had just done was idolatrous. There's no way they would have understood that. And they're good people. They love Jesus. They believe the Bible. They're exemplary citizens. But they also have some confused ideas about what it means to be a Christian and what Jesus meant when he talked about freedom. And it's not the first time would-be disciples of Jesus have been confused about freedom. After all, freedom's just another word for ... what?

Jesus famously said, "You will know the truth, and the truth will make you free" (John 8:32). Great! But what does that mean? Most people seem to think that Jesus just dropped that platitude on us out of nowhere and without any particular context, as if it were purely a stand-alone proverb. Taken out of its particular context, "the truth will set you free" can mean almost anything. In other words, it collapses into cliché. That's the problem with the bumper-sticker approach to the Bible—preaching devolves into sloganeering. Without proper context we end up with empty cliché—nice-sounding bits of nothing. Nothing is truer than "Jesus saves," but divorced from any real context, it's little more than Christian graffiti. So if someone says, "The truth will set you free from drug addiction" (or whatever), I completely agree. But I hasten to add that it's not what Jesus was talking about in John 8. Jesus was actually talking about being set free from a particular enslavement. But we haven't seen this.

We just pick out "The truth will set you free," carve it on a library, and carry on. Christ tamed to cliché. Truth made generic. Jesus dispensing platitudes. It wasn't until I spent seven months reading John 8 aloud on my knees every day that I began to comprehend that what Jesus was saying was deeply subversive, truly liberating, and a million miles away from empty cliché!

The first thing we need to notice about John 8 is that it is bracketed by two attempted stonings. This is significant. The chapter opens with the Pharisees wanting to stone an adulterous woman and closes with the crowd attempting to stone Jesus. In John 8, it's like Bob Dylan said, "Everybody must get stoned."[1] But why the bookends of attempted stonings? The ancient practice of stoning people to death provides an important context for what Jesus has to say in this chapter. So let's consider stoning.

As the Pharisees pointed out, the Torah did prescribe stoning for certain cases of adultery (see Deut. 22:13–24). Stoning was also the means of execution for other violations of the Torah, including blasphemy, witchcraft, Sabbath breaking, and rebellion against parents. (That Jesus refused to endorse the barbaric practice of capital punishment is highly significant, but not my main point.) The Pharisees could rightly say, "In the law Moses commanded us to stone such women" (John 8:5). But my question is simply this: Why stoning? There are certainly more efficient ways of executing a person than by a group of people throwing rocks at the condemned. If there is anything we humans have proven ourselves to be efficient at, it's killing people. Stoning is certainly not the most efficient way to kill, but it does have a couple of advantages over most other forms of public execution. First, stoning enables the entire community to participate in the killing. Second, stoning allows the individual to exonerate himself. Everyone throws a rock, so everyone participates. But the individual is allowed to tell himself, "It wasn't me who killed; I just threw one rock." In other words, stoning is a way for the community to participate in collective murder and lie to itself about it. And there you have it. Collective murder and the lies we tells ourselves about it—*this* is the context for what Jesus has to say about truth and freedom!

In talking about truth and freedom, Jesus was addressing "the Jews who had believed in him" (John 8:31). Presumably these are Judeans who had recently come to believe that Jesus was the Messiah. Jesus's ministry had been primarily in Galilee, but now Judeans from the capital city of Jerusalem were beginning to believe in the prophet from Nazareth. These new would-be disciples had come to believe that Jesus was indeed the Messiah, Israel's true King. But Jesus appeared to have been somewhat skeptical of their belief, for he said to them, "If you continue in my word, you are truly my disciples; and you will know the truth, and the truth will make you free" (John 8:31–32). Jesus was essentially saying, "Well, it's great that you've signed up to be my disciples and all, but if you stick with what I've been teaching, it will open up your eyes to some things that you need to be set free from." In the background of this conversation were conflicting ideas of what it meant to be the Jewish Messiah. Was Jesus going to lead them in their war of independence and start killing Romans to get rid of taxation without representation or was he up to something else? How did these newbie disciples of Jesus respond to what Jesus said about truth and freedom? Not so well.

> They answered him, "We are descendants of
> Abraham and have never been slaves to anyone.
> What do you mean by saying, "You will be made
> free"? (John 8:33)

Uh-oh! These brand-new disciples were already off on the wrong foot with Jesus. As soon as Jesus brought up the subject of freedom, they said, "I'm proud to be an Israelite, where at least I know I'm free!" Or something like that. Jesus said to the would-be disciples, "You need to be set free." The would-be disciples retorted, "We are free!" Obviously they were not on the same page. And by the time the whole scenario played out, the crowd was so offended at Jesus that they sought to stone him. So much for being Jesus's disciples! It should be readily apparent that the truth Jesus wanted these Judeans to see was no conventional truth of generic platitude. The truth Jesus was talking about in John 8 was so controversial that it incited the crowd first to insult and finally to violence.

For the Judean crowd gathering around Jesus, freedom was something primarily *political*. Their essential idea of freedom was that it was a form of power, especially power over and against national enemies. To come straight out and say it, freedom was a euphemism for lethal power—the power to *kill*. When you had power to kill your enemies and the will to do so, you were "free." When you had the biggest, most well-trained, best-equipped, most lethal military—then you were "free." But it's not freedom in the form of lethal power that Jesus sees as true freedom. For Jesus, freedom is liberation from sin—especially the particular sin of collective killing. Do you think I'm overreaching to make this point?

Am I inserting my own ideas into the text? Have I arbitrarily identified collective killing as the sin Jesus was talking about in John
8? Hardly! Listen to what Jesus said to the Judeans in response to
their protest that they are freedom-loving children of Abraham and
notice how Jesus brings up the issue of killing: "I know you are
descendents of Abraham; yet you look for an opportunity to kill me,
because there is no place in you for my word" (John 8:37).

This was quite shocking. Jesus had just told a group of prospec-
tive disciples that they were actually looking for an opportunity to
kill him! Why? Because collective killing *is* the sin Jesus told the
crowd they were enslaved to and needed to be set free from. Think
about that. If the crowd had taken in Jesus's words, they would
have understood that killing is incompatible with the way Jesus
was leading them. Jesus knew that what lies at the foundation of
the crowd's understanding of "freedom" was violence and murder.
For the crowd, *freedom* was just another word for having the power
to kill their enemies. The crowd said, "We're talking about freedom," but Jesus said, "No, you're talking about killing." Jesus was
unmasking what lay behind the crowd's euphemistic use of words
like *freedom*. Jesus was telling them a truth about themselves that
had long been hidden from them—a truth they really don't want
to know. Jesus also understood that in revealing this truth to the
crowd, he would become their enemy and they would seek to kill
him. And what happened? By the end of the chapter the crowd
was seeking to stone Jesus. Six months later they cried out for his
crucifixion.

It is not a popular truth that Jesus was offering … but if you can
receive it, it will set you free.

The truth that Jesus was trying to show the nationalistic crowd of Judean disciples is that freedom attained and maintained by killing is another name for slavery! Let that sink in. What they think makes them free actually enslaves them. They are slaves to their practice of collective killing for the sake of power and they self-deceptively call it freedom. For the crowd, *freedom* was just another word for *killing*. For Jesus, *freedom* was another word for *love*. Obviously they were going to be at odds. Here is the question: Is freedom just another word for the power to kill, or is freedom just another word for the choice to love? Again, do you think I'm reading this matter of killing into the text? Not at all! Let's continue with John's gospel text.

> They answered him, "Abraham is our father." Jesus said to them, "If you were Abraham's children, you would be doing what Abraham did, but now you are trying to kill me, a man who has told you the truth that I heard from God. This is not what Abraham did." (John 8:39–40)

Notice how Jesus kept turning the conversation to the subject of killing. Yes, it *is* an unpleasant subject, but we need to trust that Jesus knew what he was doing—he was trying to set us free! When the crowd again asserted that they were the children of Abraham, Jesus dismissed their claim by saying that if they were really Abraham's children, they would not be trying to kill him. Jesus then pointedly said, "This is not what Abraham did."

Let's pause for a moment and ask ourselves, "What *did* Abraham do?" We know that Abraham heard the call of God, left the city of

Ur, journeyed to a promised land, and by faith, fathered a family in his old age. That is all part of Abraham's story, but Jesus was talking specifically about *killing*. What did Abraham do that Jesus was calling the crowd to imitate in regard to killing? The answer is plain and simple: Abraham put down the knife. Abraham did *not* kill his son Isaac upon the sacrificial altar at Moriah. Abraham abandoned the sacred violence of human sacrifice. Abraham put down the knife. *This is a big deal!*

We need to be careful not to read the story of the sacrifice of Isaac in an anachronistic way. As modern people we are scandalized by the idea that God would ask a father to sacrifice his son. We see it as utterly abhorrent. But Abraham's contemporaries—especially his Canaanite neighbors—would not have seen it as scandalous or abhorrent. The sacrifice of children, especially firstborn sons, was what the gods required. This was just part of the quid pro quo arrangement between humans and the gods. The firstborn would be offered to the gods to ensure future fertility. A sacrifice of blood to secure blessing. A Canaanite contemporary of Abraham may have seen a tragic irony in an old man being asked by the gods to sacrifice his long-awaited son, but they would not have seen it as scandalous. The gods can be cruel. And they're not to be trifled with. But what did Abraham think about it? It's impossible to say. We can't crawl inside Abraham's psyche. All we know is that Abraham journeyed three days to Moriah to offer his son Isaac as a burnt offering, *all the while maintaining some kind of trust in his mysterious and newly discovered God*. Abraham was making discoveries about the nature of the divine that would in time change the whole trajectory of religion.

The episode of Moriah—what Christians call "the sacrifice of Isaac" and what Jews more accurately call "the binding of Isaac" (the *Akedah*)—is the subject of much rich and varied interpretation. But one important way of understanding the *Akedah* is that it is Abraham gaining the revelation that God does not want human sacrifice. This is a new trajectory for worship. At Moriah human sacrifice met its Waterloo—at least as a rite for what will become the Hebrew people. If Abraham is the father of monotheism, Abraham is also the father of the abolition of human sacrifice. When Abraham laid down the knife on Moriah and offered a ram instead of his son, humanity took a huge step in the right direction. (A thousand years later the Hebrew prophet Hosea would announce that God does not desire sacrifice *at all*—something Jesus twice affirmed. See Hosea 6:6, Matt. 9:13, and Matt. 12:7.) In other words, Abraham abandoned the idea of killing in the name of God. *This* is what Jesus was talking about! *This* is what Abraham did! *This* is why Jesus told the crowd that if they were truly Abraham's children they would do what Abraham did and not seek to kill in the name of God.

Yet Jesus and the Judean disciples were quickly arriving at an impasse. The real problem was that Jesus and the Judeans had such divergent ideas about God. Their ideas about God were so divergent that they were really two different beings—one was the *Abba* of Jesus; the other is the satan. Jesus said to the Judeans, "I speak of what I have seen with my Father, and you do what you have heard from your father" (John 8:38 ESV). The Father of Jesus is a preserver of life; the father of the crowd is a killer. Jesus was desperately trying to show them that God was not as they had imagined him. God is not a killer demanding blood sacrifices. God is not a war deity sanctioning the slaughter of enemies. The freedom that comes from God is not power to kill, but the choice to love. For Jesus, freedom is another word for what Abraham did when he laid down the knife and chose not to kill his son. Now Jesus was ready to unleash the hard truth that could set them free.

> "You are indeed doing what your father does." They said to him, "We are not illegitimate children; we have one father, God himself." Jesus said to them, "If God were your father, you would love me, for I came from God and now I am here. I did not come on my own, but he sent me." (John 8:41–42)

Jesus understood that he had been sent by his Father, the true and living God, to liberate humanity from false ideas about God—including the lie that God wants or sanctions killing of any kind. But for the most part, even would-be disciples were not willing to engage in a wholesale reevaluation of God if it undermined the basic foundation of the world. We can almost hear the frustration in Jesus's voice when he said to his hearers, "Why do you not understand what I say? It is because you cannot bear to hear my word" (John 8:43 ESV).

We really do not want to hear that God is calling us to rethink what it means to be free. In his debate with the Judeans, Jesus constantly juxtaposed love and killing and showed that only one correlates with true freedom. But we can hardly bear to hear that freedom can never be achieved by killing our enemies. It flies in the face of everything we've been taught to honor and cherish. Jesus knows that most of the time, most people cannot bear to be told that killing in the name of freedom is just another word for being a slave to systemic sin! (At this point some readers are quite likely to close this book and never open it again ... but I hope you will press on.)

The crowd's response to what Jesus was saying was to insinuate a vulgar insult. "We are not illegitimate children." That is their thinly disguised way of saying, "We've heard about the questionable circumstances of *your* birth; but we're not bastards ... like some around here." Things were starting to get ugly! Remember, these were people who a bit earlier had professed they wanted to be disciples of Jesus, and now they were calling their rabbi ugly names! At last Jesus dared to speak the whole truth and let the chips fall where they may.

> You are from your father the devil, and you choose to do your father's desires. He was a murderer from the beginning and does not stand in the truth, because there is no truth in him. When he lies, he speaks according to his own nature, for he is a liar and the father of lies. But because I tell you the truth, you do not believe me. (John 8:44–45)

Now we are getting to the heart of the matter. Jesus was pulling back the curtain on dark things "hidden from the foundation of the world." Jesus boldly told the Judeans that in holding to a false violence-based freedom instead of true love-based freedom, they were of their father the devil. They were not children of Abraham or children of God; they were, sadly, children of the devil. Hard words. Jesus submitted as conclusive evidence for their relationship to the devil their share in their dark father's desire to kill and lie about it. Jesus described the devil—the author of false freedom—as "a murderer from the beginning" and "the father of lies." But how was the devil a murderer from the beginning? What beginning was Jesus talking about? Obviously it is the beginning of murder itself—which is also the beginning of human civilization. We're again back at the Cain and Abel story.

The satan was present in the Cain and Abel story—stirring up rivalry and accusation, instigating violence and murder, and lying about it. With satanic ideas crawling around inside his head, Cain thought he couldn't be free until he imposed his will upon his brother. Cain, the tiller of the ground, could not share the land with his brother, the tender of flocks. Something had to give. Cain had to be free. Free from having to love his brother, free from having to care for his brother, free from having to share the land with his brother. Doing the will of his satanic father, Cain reclassified his brother as an enemy. Cain killed Abel. Cain lied to himself about it. Then Cain went forth with hands full of blood and a head full of lies to found human civilization.

The pattern was established. When competition arises with our neighbors, we will call them enemies, kill them, and tell ourselves lies about it. We will justify our killing in the name of freedom and hide the bodies behind myths and monuments, anthems and altars. We will tell ourselves the lie: "We are not our brothers' keepers. They are not our brothers. They are not 'us.' They are 'them.' They are enemies. For the sake of our rights, our land, our nation, our honor, our security, our freedom, they had to be killed." And we sing, "I'm proud to be a [fill in the blank] where at least I know I'm free." And then we make the grand pronouncement, "God bless the USA [or the Pax Romana or the Bar Kokhba revolt]." And we do it all in the name of "freedom." Except Jesus says that kind of freedom comes from the father of lies. It's this satanic freedom that Jesus wants to set us free from. As you can see, the crowd did not attempt to stone Jesus for positing generic platitudes about nebulous truth and freedom. The crowd wanted to stone Jesus for pulling back the covers on their dark tryst with the devil!

> Which of you convicts me of sin? If I tell the truth,
> why do you not believe me? Whoever is from God
> hears the words of God. The reason you do not hear
> them is that you are not from God. (John 8:46–47)

Jesus began this discourse by saying, "I am the light of the world. Whoever follows me will not walk in darkness but will have the light of life" (John 8:12). Jesus is completely free from the darkness of the Cain system of collective murder and the lies we tell ourselves about it. As the light of the world, Jesus shines the light of truth on the dark system of violence that lies at the foundation of the world. Unlike most of us, Jesus is not implicated in the human system of violence. Jesus is untainted by the legacy of Cain's city. Actually, the only way to be fully free from complicity in our systems of violence is to embrace a radical prophetic poverty—the kind we find in the saintly lives of those like St. Francis and Mother Teresa. Admittedly, most of us cannot fully emulate their radical poverty, but it is from such lives that light shines on our dark foundations. This light enables us to at least recognize our complicity in violence and to seek a better way.

Jesus as the light of the world is completely innocent of all complicity with systemic sin—so much so that he boldly asked, "Which of you convicts me of sin?" Jesus cannot be indicted in the systems of foundational murder and the accompanying self-deception. But this very thing guaranteed Jesus would become a victim of the system. Violence cannot tolerate the presence of one who owes it nothing. It's why everyone at a stoning needs to throw a rock. If someone at a stoning doesn't participate, they are in danger of becoming the next victim. For the illusion of innocence to work, everyone must participate in the collective murder. The one who won't throw a rock becomes a prophet shining light on the evil of stoning. The community must then either repent or stone the prophet.

On his final visit to Jerusalem, Jesus lamented, "Jerusalem, Jerusalem, the city that kills the prophets and stones those who are sent to it!" (Matt. 23:37). Of course, in the end, Jesus was also killed. But his death is what shames the whole system of "redemptive violence." We come to realize that in using violence as a means of achieving justice, we are capable of murdering God! The whole evil system is dragged into the light and exposed for what it is. Seen in the light of the resurrection, the crucifixion of Jesus demands that we once and for all renounce violence as a means of achieving just ends.

> The Jews answered him, "Are we not right in saying
> that you are a Samaritan and have a demon?" (John
> 8:48)

Now all pretense of civil discourse had been abandoned. These Judeans were decidedly *not* going to become disciples of Jesus. In their rage they leveled two accusations at Jesus. Revealingly, they accused Jesus of belonging to a despised ethnic minority, and ironically, they accused Jesus of having a demon. These erstwhile disciples had returned to the dead-end cul-de-sac of hatred and hostility. They were slinking back into the very darkness that Jesus tried to rescue them from. In accusing Jesus of having a demon, they unwittingly revealed that *they* were the ones under demonic sway. Instead of embracing the truth that would set them free, the Judeans consoled themselves in the chains of racism and witch hunts. Jesus concluded his debate with the failed Judean disciples by speaking of Abraham in whom they took such national pride.

> "Your ancestor Abraham rejoiced that he would see my day; he saw it and was glad." Then the Jews said to him, "You are not yet fifty years old, and you have seen Abraham?" Jesus said to them, "Very truly, I tell you, before Abraham was, I am." So they picked up stones to throw at him, but Jesus hid himself and went out of the temple. (John 8:56–59)

For the second time that day, the stones of execution were ready to fly. Indeed, an angry crowd is the most dangerous thing in the world! What finally sent the crowd over the edge was Jesus's claim that he was what Abraham was looking for. Abraham was looking for a city not built by Cain. Abraham was looking for a city whose architect was God. Abraham was looking for a way out of the vicious cycle of reciprocal violence masquerading under the guise of freedom. Abraham was looking for a way of structuring human civilization that came not from the satan but from the eternal I AM. What Abraham was looking for, and by faith had caught a fleeting glimpse of, was what Jesus was bringing! Jesus was bringing the reign and rule of God where freedom would not be a cover for killing but an expression of self-giving love.

When your city is built upon violence, freedom is just another word for killing your brother. But when your city is built upon love, freedom is just another word for being your brother's keeper.

Jesus brings us the truth that will set us free. The truth is that God is love and light. The truth is that our enemies are really our alienated brothers. The truth is there is no "them"—there is only us. The truth is that freedom is love, not power. The truth is there is another way to arrange human civilization than what we have known. The truth is that the way of war is a lie. It comes from the father of lies, the father of murder. James Carroll in his important book *Jerusalem, Jerusalem* asks this penetrating question:

> War is a given fact of the human condition. But is it true? … The traditional narrative suggests that the solution to violence is more violence. Not only that, but violence as a source of meaning and valor. Violence can be sanctified as sacrifice and atonement, as the will of God. But is *that* true?[2]

Jesus answers Carroll's question with an emphatic no. It's not true. It's a lie. War does *not* have to be a given fact. Violence does *not* have to be the source of meaning and valor. Violence is *not* the will of God! Jesus is unambiguous in his renunciation of the lie that true freedom can be attained by violence. Jesus offers us his truth to save us from Satan's hideous lie. But we must have the courage to step out of the false security of the darkness and into the liberating light of freedom redefined. The truth is: God is love and our enemies are our brothers. Freedom is just another word for what happens to us when we live in the light of that truth. Do we have the courage to embrace the truth that will set us free? Or would we rather keep throwing rocks at those who tell us that the way of war and violence is a lie that keeps us enslaved to sin and Satan?

If we carefully examine how we use the word *freedom*, it becomes apparent that we use it to sanction our perceived right to pursue happiness in a self-interested fashion. We want the freedom to arrange the world in such a way that it serves the interest of our own self or our own group. But that is not freedom. That is the way to slavery and self-destruction. More than a century ago, Fyodor Dostoevsky saw through the self-deceptive way we use the word *freedom*, when he wrote:

> The world has proclaimed freedom, especially of late, but what do we see in this freedom of theirs: only slavery and suicide! For the world says: "You have needs, therefore satisfy them, for you have the same rights as the noblest and richest men.

Do not be afraid to satisfy them, but even increase them"—this is the current teaching of the world. And in this they see freedom. But what comes of this right to increase one's needs? For the rich, *isolation* and spiritual suicide; for the poor, envy and murder. ... And no wonder that instead of freedom they have fallen into slavery.[3]

Dostoevsky is simply echoing what Jesus said long before him. Freedom cannot be attained by fighting for our rights. That is the way to slavery and suicide. It's the long road out of Eden that always leads us away from God. As Rowan Williams has said, "What makes us secure in the world's terms is the enemy of the transcendent God."[4] Security in the world's terms is a false security. Making ourselves an enemy of the God who is love and light is why we keep finding our way back to the man-made hells of violence inflicted in the name of somebody's freedom. As long as we keep telling ourselves that the only way forward in history is to fight yet another war in the name of freedom, we find our road circling back into the same old hell-holes that Jesus seeks to lead us out of. David Bentley Hart put it this way: "Hell is the name of that false history against which the true story, in Christ, is told, and it is exposed as the true destination of all our violence."[5]

Violence in the name of freedom always circles back to hell. Jesus is the way out. In the midst of our sanctioned practice of collective killing done in the name of freedom, Jesus comes and speaks the truth that will set us free. Or as Jesus said, "If the Son makes you free, you will be free indeed" (John 8:36). Do we really believe in the way of freedom offered to us by the Son of God?

> Do you really think the only way
> to bring about the peace
> is to sacrifice your children
> and kill all your enemies?[6]
> **—Larry Norman**

Not long ago I was in Istanbul, Turkey. While there I toured the Topkapi Palace—the former royal palace of the Ottoman sultans and center of the Ottoman Empire. Among the many artifacts collected throughout the centuries and on display was an item I found quite remarkable—the sword of the prophet Muhammad. There, under protective glass and illuminated by high-tech lighting, was the fourteen-hundred-year-old sword of the founder of Islam. As I looked at the sword with its curved handle and jeweled scabbard, I thought how significant it is that no one will ever visit a museum and be shown a weapon that belonged to Jesus. Jesus brings freedom to the world in a way different from Pharaoh, Alexander, Caesar, Muhammad, Napoleon, and Patton. Jesus sets us free not by killing enemies but by being killed by enemies and forgiving them ... by whom I mean us. Forgiveness and cosuffering love is the truth that sets us free—free from the false freedom inflicted by swords ancient and modern. Muhammad could fight a war in the name of freedom to liberate his followers from Meccan oppression, but Jesus had a radically different understanding of freedom. And lest this sound like crass Christian triumphalism, my real question is this: Do we Christians secretly wish that Jesus were more like Muhammad? It's not an idle question. The moment the church took to the Crusades in order to fight Muslims, it had already surrendered its vision of

Jesus to the model of Muhammad. Muhammad may have thought freedom could be found at the end of a sword, but Jesus never did. So are Christians who most enthusiastically support US-led wars against Muslim nations actually trying to turn Jesus into some version of Muhammad? It's a serious question. It's a serious question because freedom is just another word for … what?

CHAPTER 6

THE THINGS THAT MAKE FOR PEACE

"You're not a *pacifist* are you?" I get that question a lot. People who have read my books or heard my sermons will often confront me with that question. There seems to be a hint of scandal implied in the question, like asking, "You're not a *pornographer* are you?" This strikes me as a bit strange. I suppose the hint of scandal comes from the assumption that pacifism is a sort of cousin to cowardice. This also strikes me as strange. To endorse the dominant view that the employment of violence is compatible with Christianity requires no courage at all—that's just following the crowd. But to differ from the dominant view on the sanctity of state-sponsored violence may require an uncommon reservoir of moral conviction. Pacifism is not a popular position in America, and especially not among patriotic evangelicals who have ardently sought to amalgamate the American state and the Christian faith into one hybrid entity. Still I know what you're wondering: What's my answer to the loaded question about pacifism?

First of all, I don't like labels. Kierkegaard was right when he said, "When you label me, you negate me." Just call someone a pacifist, and you can dismiss them with a wave of your hand. Labels are often a way to avoid thinking. "Oh, he's one of *those*." Case closed. Mind closed. That being said, I have no problem with Christians who adopt the label of pacifist. If nothing else, they provide an alternative witness to that of the Christian militarist whose numbers are legion. But I actually *don't* claim the label of pacifist for this reason: pacifism is a political position on violence. It's a position one could adopt *apart* from Jesus Christ—as for example, the great writer and humanist Kurt Vonnegut did. But I am not a political pacifist. What I am is a Christian. And as a Christian, we can talk about how Christ informs humanity on the subject of violence.

In my long and winding journey, I've come to understand that to live gently in a violent world is part of the counterculture of following Christ. This is not something I would *ever* have arrived at on my own. I am not, by nature, a gentle person. For most of my life, I have viewed violence with a kind of affection. In my youth I got in plenty of fights. I enjoyed violent movies. Cowboy justice held a romantic appeal. As a pastor I supported nearly all (if not literally all) of America's military adventures. If my views on violence have changed—and they have—the blame falls squarely on Jesus! It's not like I woke up one day and said, "Hey, I think I'll adopt a position of Christian nonviolence just for the fun of it. I bet that will be popular!" No, that's not what happened. What happened was once the red, white, and blue varnish was removed from Jesus and I learned to read the Gospels free of a star-spangled interpretation, I discovered that my Lord and Savior had a lot of things to say about peace that I had been missing. I was as surprised as anyone! But once you've seen the truth, you can't unknow what you know and be true to yourself. So let's talk about it.

Jesus's triumphal entry into Jerusalem on what we now call Palm Sunday was a confusing event full of contradictions. It was an incongruent mix of cheers and tears. There was jubilation among the Passover pilgrims as they waved palm branches and shouted, "Hosanna!" Passover was the annual celebration of Israel's liberation from bondage in Egypt and the holiday had come to have strong patriotic overtones, especially for a people enduring the humiliation of a foreign occupation. Hoping that the miracle-working prophet from Galilee would turn out to be the long-awaited messiah who would liberate Israel from Roman occupation, the Passover pilgrims ecstatically shouted, "Hosanna! Liberate now!" But Jesus was obviously distressed about something. While the crowd was joyfully shouting, Jesus was weeping over Jerusalem. Quite clearly Jesus did not share the optimistic enthusiasm of the crowd. What was going on?

What was going on was that a violent, nationalistic vision of the Messiah had made it impossible for the people of Jerusalem to perceive the things that make for peace. Despite their Palm Sunday cheers, the crowd ultimately failed to recognize the Galilean Prince of Peace as Israel's true Messiah. The tragic result of this failure came a generation later with Jerusalem's total destruction and the loss of hundreds of thousands of lives. Listen again to what Jesus said as he wept over the doomed city:

> If you, even you, had only recognized on this day
> *the things that make for peace*! But now they are

hidden from your eyes. Indeed, the days will come
upon you, when your enemies will set up ramparts
around … you and your children within you, and
they will not leave within you one stone upon
another; because you did not recognize the time of
your visitation from God. (Luke 19:42–44)

On the Sunday of Jesus's arrival in Jerusalem, the crowd of
Passover pilgrims waved palm branches and shouted hosanna in a
patriotic remembrance of the Maccabean revolt two centuries earlier.
(It would be similar to how Americans remember the Revolutionary
War and celebrate the Fourth of July.) What they were clearly anticipating was that Jesus was about to do it again. Just as Judah Maccabeus
had led a Jewish war of independence against the Seleucid Empire,
now Jesus was expected to lead a war of independence against the
Roman Empire. The expectation was for Jesus to be a kind of first-
century Jewish George Washington. The prevailing sentiment was
a yearning for war, not peace. The dominant assumption was that
violence was the path that would lead to freedom. When Jesus saw
that his vision for the kingdom of God had been conscripted by
a violent nationalistic agenda, he wept and lamented the fate of
Jerusalem. The patriotic crowd wanted the second coming of Joshua
the Canaanite killer or David the Philistine slayer or Judah "The
Hammer" Maccabeus. But Jesus was not the second coming of any
Jewish war hero—he was the first coming of the Prince of Peace!
    When Jesus wept and said, "If only you had known the things
that make for peace," he wasn't talking about spiritual peace or inner
peace or emotional peace; he was talking about peace from the literal

hell that is war. Today there is a tendency to overspiritualize the way Jesus spoke of peace. By making peace primarily a privatized spiritual peace, we are free to carry the banners of war down the road and keep the world as it's always been—just one more war away from peace. (Now all we have to do is win the "war on terror" and peace will prevail. Call me dubious.)

When the peace of Christ is confined to the private realm of individual emotions, it is not taken seriously as an alternative political vision for humanity. Post-Constantine Christians have learned to be quite comfortable in claiming the peace of Christ while waging war upon their neighbors. We have made the *Pax Christus* a private affair while holding to the Pax Romana as the only way to arrange the world. But I insist this is deeply problematic for those who confess Jesus is Lord. Christians may claim that war is a necessity, but they cannot claim that Jesus endorses this idea. Jesus was quite plain in teaching that a people who won't repent of (or rethink) the worn-out idea that war is a legitimate means of making the world a better place are doomed to a horrid self-inflicted judgment. The means never justify the ends. The means are the ends in the process of becoming. If the means are violence and killing, the end will be violent death. Jesus taught this: "All who take the sword will perish by the sword" (Matt. 26:52).

Prior to his arrival in Jerusalem, Jesus had been told about some Galilean revolutionaries who had been executed by the authority of the Roman governor. Jesus's response is significant:

> Do you think that because these Galileans suffered
> in this way they were worse sinners than all other

Galileans? No, I tell you; but unless you repent, you will all perish as they did. Or those eighteen who were killed when the tower of Siloam fell on them—do you think that they were worse offenders than all the others living in Jerusalem? No, I tell you; but unless you repent, you will all perish like they did. (Luke 13:2–5)

We have become so accustomed to interpreting all of Jesus's warnings of impending judgment as references to a postmortem hell that we often screen out his actual message. (Is that our subconscious intent?) In this passage Jesus was not talking about afterlife consequences but was desperately trying to warn his fellow countrymen that if they didn't rethink their hell-bent-for-destruction desire for a war of independence, they would all perish by Roman swords and Roman catapult stones. The nation didn't repent, and that's exactly how they perished in AD 70. Jesus was offering his nation a way of peace, a way that didn't end in a self-inflicted hell. But it would require rethinking their entrenched nationalism and penchant for violent revolution. The only other alternative was for Jerusalem to be reduced to a heap of smoldering rubble littered with rotting corpses—"where their worm never dies, and the fire is never quenched" (Mark 9:48). By the time he reached Jerusalem on Palm Sunday, Jesus realized that, though his death would forestall a Jewish rebellion against Rome for a generation, eventually the drums of war would drown out his message of peace and thrust the City of Peace into the Gehenna of fire.

> Jerusalem, Jerusalem, you who kill the prophets
> and stone those sent to you, how often I have
> longed to gather your children together, as a hen
> gathers her chicks under her wings, and you were
> not willing! Look, your house is left to you deso-
> late. (Luke 13:34–35 NIV)

How sad. No wonder Jesus was weeping. But the saddest thing of all is that it didn't have to happen. Our looming Armageddons are always a possibility but never an inevitability. Armageddon is only inevitable if we listen to the propaganda that comes croaking from the dragons, beasts, and false prophets of nationalism, empire, and war. (See Rev. 16:13–16.) Jesus wept over Jerusalem because their fate could have been avoided. If they had believed in Jesus as the messianic Prince of Peace instead of a messianic Lord of War, Jerusalem could have actually become the City of Peace. Instead, they chose the path that led to a hellish nightmare of siege, famine, cannibalism, destruction, and death.

The point is this: it wasn't enough for Jerusalem to hail Jesus as the coming king—they did that! They also had to believe in the new way of peace the coming King was proclaiming. Did you catch that? It's not enough to believe in Jesus; we also have to believe in the Jesus *way*! (For that matter, I'm not quite sure what it means to "believe in Jesus" without believing in the Jesus way.) If we don't believe in the Jesus way, we won't know the things that make for peace. Then we are bound to continue down the well-worn road to Gehenna and Armageddon, to Auschwitz and Hiroshima. Quite simply, it's not enough to just believe in Jesus.

In fact, a reckless assumption that because we believe in Jesus and therefore God is on our side can actually aggravate our addiction to Armageddon. It's happened before. In America. And it led to America's bloodiest war.

Whether or not slavery was the direct cause for the first shots fired upon Fort Sumter in April of 1861 is a matter of scholarly debate. What is undeniable is that the fuel that caused the American Civil War to ignite into a conflagration that resulted in 750,000 deaths was two-and-a-half centuries of slavery. From its Jamestown beginnings, the American colonies—and later the United States— practiced one of the most brutal forms of slavery the world has ever known. The preservation of an institution that systematically dehumanized millions of people for the sake of economic gain was not a thing that made for peace! Inevitably that kind of cruel exploitation would overflow its cup and unleash death and hell, bringing everything that is the opposite of peace. During the horror of the American Civil War, the land of the free became a burning Gehenna. Thirty percent of Southern men of fighting age were slain on battlefields that saw the birth of modern warfare. From then on, war would be totalized and mechanized. The four horseman of the Apocalypse galloped across America leaving a wake of war, disease, famine, and death.

But in a tragic irony that will help make my point, a spiritual revival had swept through America during the decade before the Civil War. Americans flocked to churches and evangelistic meetings. This was especially true in the more religious South, where Christianity was embraced with greater fervency than in the less zealous North. Across the country revival was on, churches grew, conversions multiplied. People got saved, praised Jesus, and talked about heaven. Then they went to hell. Or at least the same kind of hell Jesus had warned Jerusalem about during his final days. Despite a great revival, a nation of Christians was thrust into a hell of cannonballs, Gatling guns, field hospitals, and amputation saws. Great cities were set aflame and fields were littered with thousands of rotting corpses. The fires were not quenched and the maggots did not die.

What had gone wrong? Millions had accepted Jesus and shouted hosanna, but they did not know the things that make for peace. They prayed a sinner's prayer, "got right with God," and kept their slaves. They had a faith that would justify the slave owner while bringing no justice to the slave. They had faith that gave them a ticket to heaven and a highway to hell. The religious fervor in the conservative churches of the South only served to convince them that they were blessed by heaven. They were quite certain God smiled upon their deep devotion to their southern-fried Jesus. If they had to go to war to preserve their freedom, so be it—God was on their side. They were sure of it. But there would be hell to pay.

To help you comprehend how wrong the conservative churches of the Antebellum South were despite flaunting their faith in Jesus and clutching their well-worn Bibles, I'm going to enlist the help of someone who was there and saw it all—Mark Twain. In the chapter entitled "You Can't Pray a Lie" in Twain's beloved novel *Adventures of Huckleberry Finn*, Huck Finn has helped hide Miss Watson's runaway slave, Jim. But Huck *thought* he was committing a sin in helping a runaway slave. Huck had learned in Sunday school "that people that acts as I'd been acting ... goes to everlasting fire." So in an act of repentance in order to save his soul, Huck wrote a note to Miss Watson and told her where she could find her runaway slave. Now Huck was ready to pray his "sinner's prayer" and "get saved."

I felt good and all washed clean of sin for the first time I had ever felt so in my life, and I knowed I could pray now. But I didn't do it straight off but laid the paper down and set there thinking— thinking how good it was all this happened so, and how near I come to being lost and going to hell. And went on thinking. And got to thinking over our trip down the river; and I see Jim before me all the time: in the day and in the night-time, sometimes moonlight, sometimes storms, and we a-floating along, talking and singing and laughing. But somehow I couldn't seem to strike no places to harden me against him, but only the other kind. I'd see him standing my watch on top of his'n, 'stead of calling me, so I could go on sleeping; and see how glad he was when I come back out of the fog; and when I come to him again in the swamp, up there where the feud was; and such-like times; and would always call me honey and pet me and do everything he could think of for me, and how good he always was; and at last I struck the time I saved him by telling the men we had smallpox aboard, and he was so grateful, and said I was the best friend old Jim ever had in the world and the *only* he's got now; and then I happened to look around and see the paper. It was a close place. I took it up, and held it in my hand. I was a-trembling, because I'd got to decide, forever, betwixt two things, and I knowed it. I studied a minute, sort of holding my breath, and then says to myself: "All right, then, I'll go to hell"—and tore it up. It was awful thoughts and awful words but they was said. And I let them stay said; and never thought no more about reforming.[1]

Huck Finn had been shaped by the Christianity he'd found in his Missouri Sunday school—a Christianity focused on heaven in the afterlife while preserving the status quo of the here and now. Huck thought that helping Jim escape from slavery was a sin, because that's what he had been taught. He knew he couldn't ask God to forgive him until he was ready to "repent" and betray Jim. Huck didn't want to go to hell; he wanted to be saved. But Huck loved his friend more, so he was willing to go to hell in order to save his friend from slavery.

Twain did a masterful job of showing us how wrongheaded Christians can be about what constitutes salvation. For Huck to act according to justice, he had to *think* he was committing a great sin. For Huck to act Christlike, he had to *think* he was forsaking Christianity. For Huck to love his neighbor as himself, he had to *think* he was condemning his soul to hell. Think about that a while!

Mark Twain used his skillful pen to skewer the conservative Christianity of the American South. Though Mark Twain wasn't a believing Christian (and he wasn't)—he *was* a prophet to the prevailing Christianity of his day. This was a compromised Christianity in desperate need of a prophetic voice. In seeking to preserve an economy dependent upon slave labor, Southern churches had embraced a fatally distorted faith. Probably without even knowing what they were doing, these Christians had quite effectively used Jesus and the Bible to validate their racist assumptions and protect their vested interests. They went to church on Sunday. They got saved. They loved Jesus. They waved their palms and shouted hosanna on Palm Sunday. But like the crowd in Jerusalem eighteen centuries earlier, they didn't know the things that made for peace. And Jesus wept over an America headed to hell. The churches were full and slavery continued—until the Civil War, that is. Then 750,000 people died for the sins of America.

This is more than a recitation of history; there's a lesson to learn here. When we don't know the things that make for peace, we can barrel down the highway to hell, all the while singing about how much we love Jesus and how wonderful it is to be saved. This should disturb us. How can it be that generations of religiously observant people can say all the right things about Jesus and still be on the wrong road? How can we know the things that make for a good church service but not know the things that make for peace?

Jesus said that something has hidden the peaceful way from our eyes ... and more often than not, it's a flag. If patriotism simply means the pride of place that inspires civic responsibility, so be it. But if patriotism means "my country right or wrong," it's a kind of groupthink blindness that hides the things that make for peace. Unfurled flags of nationalism have a long history of hiding the things of Christ that make for peace. Whether they are Roman, Byzantine, Spanish, French, English, German, Russian, or American flags, when they hide the things that make for peace, they are no longer the innocent banners of a benign patriotism.

So what are the things that make for peace? What is it we need to perceive if we are to avoid the bloody boomerang of a self-inflicted hell? Jesus told us when he said:

> In everything do to others as you would have them do to you; for this is the law and the prophets. Enter through the narrow gate; for the gate is wide and the road is easy that leads to destruction, and there are many who take it. For the gate is narrow and the road is hard that leads to life, and there are few who find it. (Matt. 7:12–14)

The things that make for peace are the two great commandments: love of God and love of neighbor, but especially the second command. (Love of God is only validated by a cosuffering love of neighbor.) The "golden rule" of evaluating our actions through the eyes of our neighbor is the narrow and difficult road that leads to life and peace. The golden rule *is* the narrow gate. The narrow gate is not a sinner's prayer; the narrow gate is the practice of the Jesus way. The narrow gate is fulfilling the law and the prophets by empathetic love of neighbor in imitation of Jesus. When we hate and vilify others for ideological reasons, when we demonize and dehumanize others for nationalistic reasons, when we use and exploit others for economic reasons, we are on the highway to hell—we have chosen the well-worn road that leads to war and destruction. The deeply disconcerting thing is that it is entirely possible to cruise down the broad road of impending doom while singing songs of praise to Jesus. It happened on the first Palm Sunday. It happened a hundred and fifty years ago in America. It continues to happen today. If we think Jesus shares and endorses our disdain and enmity for our enemies, we don't know the things that make for peace, and we are headed for an inevitable destruction, even if it takes a generation or two to arrive at our horrible destination. If we console ourselves with the promise of heaven in the afterlife while creating hell in this present life, we have embraced the tawdry religion of the crusader and forsaken the true faith of our Savior.

The road of nonviolent peacemaking is not an easy road, it's not a popular road, and it's certainly not a road for cowards. The road of "God is on our side, and he shall surely smite our enemies" is a wide road. A lot of parades have gone down that road. It doesn't take much courage to travel that road; just fall in step and follow the crowd. A marching band is usually playing. But it's also the road that leads to burned villages, bombed cities, and solemn processions of flag-draped coffins. Until the self-professed followers of Jesus are willing to forsake the wide road for the narrow way, the popular sentiment for the unpopular conviction, the easy assumptions for the hard alternatives—Jesus will continue to weep while his disciples shout hosanna.

I won't pretend I have perfected the art of following Jesus on the narrow way that leads to life and peace instead of traipsing down the broad way that leads to death and war. Far from it. I'm a newcomer to the steep and narrow path of peacemaking. If I'm not careful, I can find myself trying to climb the path of peacemaking in a far too unpeaceable way. Which means I am falling on my face—or even tumbling back down the steep path. But still I know it's the right path. I would not have found, much less chosen to travel, this hard and demanding path unless Jesus had led me on to it. I wasn't going to be led onto the path of peacemaking by Gandhi or Rumi—as admirable as those men were. If today I'm trying to walk the narrow path of nonviolent peacemaking, its only because its where I find the footsteps of Jesus. It's an uncrowded path, perhaps at times a lonely path. But it's worth traveling, because I keep catching glimpses of Jesus farther up the road.

O God, you have made of one blood all the
peoples of the earth, and sent your blessed Son to
preach peace to those who are far off and to those
who are near: Grant that people everywhere may
seek after you and find you; bring the nations into
your fold; pour out your Spirit upon all flesh,
and hasten the coming of your kingdom;
through Jesus Christ our Lord. *Amen.*

—*The Book of Common Prayer*

CHAPTER 7

CLOUDS, CHRIST, AND KINGDOM COME

We live in a political world
Where peace is not welcome at all
It's turned away from the door
to wander some more
Or put up against the wall

We live in a political world
Everything is hers or his
Climb into the frame and shout God's name
But you're never sure what it is[1]
—Bob Dylan, "Political World"

Recently I was interviewed by a popular Christian blogger who was interested in my theological journey. Apparently some people are curious as to why a "successful" pastor would adopt a new theological trajectory—especially if it's perceived as a risky move. The interview was published on the blog site under the title "From Word of Faith to Church Fathers: A Conversation with Brian Zahnd." Anyway, I enjoyed our conversation. The interviewer's final question was this: "What would you say has been the most revolutionary insight you've come to since you started this journey?" Here is the answer I gave:

> The revolutionary insight that's been central to my theological journey is a deeper understanding of what the kingdom of God actually is.
>
> I remember telling my church eight years ago that seeing the kingdom of God had given me "new eyes." Reading the Bible with "kingdom eyes" made Scripture brand new to me. I came to realize that the kingdom of God was virtually the sole topic of Jesus' teaching ministry. The gospel of the kingdom is what the apostles were announcing in the book of Acts. And even though Paul doesn't often use the term "kingdom of God" in his epistles, I came to understand that what Jesus tends to call the kingdom of God, Paul tends to call salvation, *but they're talking about the same thing*!
>
> In 2006 I worked on this single question for several months: *What is salvation?* I finally concluded that this is the best answer: *Salvation is the kingdom of God.* Our personal experience with the kingdom of God (including forgiveness) is our personal experience of salvation, but the kingdom of God is much bigger than our personal experience

of it. The problem we have today is that the term "kingdom of God" is archaic and obscured under layers of religious veneer. "Kingdoms" went out with the Middle Ages and we tend to think of the "kingdom of God/heaven" as privatized Christianity experienced in our personal spiritual lives.

But Jesus was [doing something far more radical when He proclaimed the kingdom of God—he was announcing] that the government of God was at long last being established in the world through what He was doing … in light of this, we need to rethink our lives and begin to live under the administration of Christ.

This kingdom paradigm revolutionized my theology—soteriology, eschatology, ecclesiology, and political theology *all* had to be reworked under the rubric of the kingdom of God. So today when I make the seminal Christian confession "Jesus is Lord," I'm not just expressing something about my personal spiritual life; I'm also making a revolutionary political statement. And that's a game-changer![2]

Perceiving the kingdom of God as an actual political reality is a game changer. Once you see that Jesus has his own political agenda, his own vision for arranging human society, his own criteria for judging nations, then it's impossible to give your heart and soul to the power-based, win-at-all-costs partisan politics that call for our allegiance. Unfortunately, what I've learned through bitter experience is that a lot of people don't want the game changed. They want to *win* the game—not *change* the game. My most vehement critics tend to come from those who regard my deep ambivalence toward a political "take back America for God" agenda as a scandalous betrayal. They simply cannot imagine how God's will is going to be done if "our side" doesn't win the political game. This is the game most of the church has played for seventeen centuries—use Christianity to endorse or buttress a particular political agenda. *Christian* then becomes a mere adjective to the dominant political noun. What is dominant is a particular political agenda. Politics trumps everything. The political tail wags the Christian dog. Christianity's role is to serve a political agenda. So viewed through the American lens, Christianity is seen to endorse democracy and capitalism, just as it was once seen in Europe to endorse monarchy and feudalism. To even suggest that Jesus doesn't necessarily endorse every aspect of Jeffersonian democracy and laissez-faire capitalism is enough to get you burned at the stake (hopefully only in a metaphorical sense).

The problem with the chaplaincy view of Christianity is the assumption that the kingdom (government) of God has yet to come. If we think the kingdom of God is still waiting in the wings, then our political allegiance is given to one of the players currently on stage. Christianity becomes subservient to conventional political power, a chaplain to offer innocuous invocations, a lackey to hand out "Christian voter guides."

But what if the whole assumption is wrong? What if the reign of Christ over the nations has already begun? What if the politics of God are already present? What if the age to come has already been inaugurated (even if far from fully established)? What if Jesus has no interest in endorsing some other political agenda *because he has his own*?! That would change everything. And it's clearly what Jesus believed about what he was doing! If we learn to read the Gospels free from the Constantinian assumption that the kingdom of God has not yet dawned, we will find a fresh, new story. If we let the Gospels speak for themselves instead of hammering them into a sword for our favorite empire, we would see a radical alternative. Once we stop trying to use Jesus to endorse monarchy or democracy, feudalism or capitalism, it becomes quite clear that Jesus was announcing the arrival of the reign and rule of God through what he was doing. Jesus had been hinting at this throughout his teaching ministry, but on the night before his crucifixion, he began to speak explicitly about it. But do we have ears to hear? Let's try.

After the Last Supper with his disciples, Jesus was arrested in the garden of Gethsemane and brought before the Sanhedrin for a late-night interrogation by the high priest Caiaphas. As Jesus remained silent during the examination, Caiaphas grew frustrated, eventually saying, "I put you under oath before the living God, tell us if you are the Messiah, the Son of God" (Matt. 26:63). Jesus's response is extraordinarily significant.

> You have said so. But I tell you,
>> From now on you will see the Son of Man
>> seated at the right hand of Power
>> and coming on the clouds of heaven. (Matt. 26:64)

Listen carefully to what Jesus told Caiaphas. After Jesus acknowledged that he was indeed Israel's Messiah, he added that he was also
the mysterious Son of Man and that Caiaphas would *from now on*
see the Son of Man seated at the right hand of God and coming in
the clouds of heaven. The phrase *from now on* should make it quite
clear that Jesus was not primarily talking about his Second Coming.
Jesus was not referencing something that would take place way off
in the future but something that was coming to pass in the present
moment, something contemporary with Caiaphas. Recognizing this
is a big deal—a game changer! Unfortunately, we have been so con-
ditioned to hear all of Jesus's "when the Son of Man comes" language
as a reference to a far distant "second coming" that we fail to realize
that most of the time Jesus was talking about the reign of God he
was establishing there and then. For example, Jesus told his disciples
that when the Son of Man comes, "he will dress himself for service
and have them recline at table, and he will come and serve them"
(Luke 12:37 ESV). This is exactly what happened in the Upper Room
on the eve of Jesus's suffering! Jesus girded himself with a towel,
assumed the role of a servant, and washed his disciples' feet (John
13:1–17). It was a dramatic way for him to fulfill his own prophecy
and announce the coming of the Son of Man and the long-awaited
reign of God. The Son of Man was coming! Right there! Right then!
But what does the coming of the Son of Man mean?

The Son of Man as an eschatological or end-times figure
originated in the apocalyptic book of Daniel and was enormously
influential on how Jesus understood what he was doing. (Jesus
referred to the Son of Man no less than eighty times). In chapter
seven of the book, Daniel had a dream where he saw a series of beasts

coming up from the sea and wreaking havoc on earth. The first beast was like a lion, the second like a bear, the third like a leopard, the fourth a monstrous creature. These beasts represented the succession of arrogant empires throughout history that would use military might to shape the world according to their own selfish agenda and fill the world with suffering. (These beasts are generally associated with the historic empires of Babylon, Persia, Greece, and Rome.) But then, as is typical in dreams, the perspective suddenly changed, and Daniel found himself a spectator in the court of heaven. God, as the Ancient of Days, was presiding and was ready to issue a judgment on behalf of a world oppressed by these beastly empires.

> I saw in the night visions,
> and behold, with the clouds of heaven
>   there came one like a son of man,
> and he came to the Ancient of Days
>   and was presented before him.
> And to him was given dominion
>   and glory and a kingdom,
> that all peoples, nations, and languages
>   should serve him;
> his dominion is an everlasting dominion,
>   which shall not pass away,
> and his kingdom one
>   that shall not be destroyed. (Dan. 7:13–14 ESV)

Daniel had first been shown how beastly empires through their military might would dominate the nations for greedy purposes.

Then, from a new vantage point in heaven, Daniel saw the intervention of the Ancient of Days. A human being (not a beast) called the Son of Man *ascended* from the earth into the clouds of heaven to stand before the Ancient of Days. This Son of Man was given dominion over all peoples, nations, and languages. The court of heaven announced that the kingdom of the Son of Man would never pass away or be destroyed. That was the vision. It was the hopeful vision that someday a human being would ascend from earth to heaven, be seated at the right hand of the Ancient of Days, and be given dominion over the nations. It was in this way that humanity would be liberated from the oppression of an endless parade of beastly empires.

Daniel's dream was that the Son of Man ascended *up* into the clouds of heaven and was given dominion over the nations. It was this vision that shaped both the apocalyptic expectations of first-century Jews and informed Jesus's understanding of his identity and vocation. Jesus saw himself as the Son of Man who would receive dominion over the nations and liberate the world from the tyranny of military empires. But he would not attain this dominion through violence *for that would make him just another beast!* (This was the essence of the third wilderness temptation: to bow down to Satan in order to receive dominion over the nations. It was the temptation to become the latest Pharaoh, the latest Caesar, the latest beast.) No, Jesus would not be a violent beast; he would be the glorious Son of Man.

When Jesus was on trial before Caiaphas, he claimed to be *that* Son of Man. Jesus told Caiaphas that from now on, Caiaphas would see the Son of Man installed as King over the nations, coming before

God the Father in the clouds of heaven and given an everlasting dominion. Jesus claimed to be *that* King. This is why Caiaphas tore his robes and cried, "Blasphemy!"

Jesus was condemned to death by both Caiaphas and Pilate for the *same reason*—he claimed to be a king. Not a "spiritual king" over a "spiritual kingdom" but a real king over a political kingdom—but a very different kind of political kingdom. It is a kingdom that you have to be born again to even perceive, as Jesus told Nicodemus. And as Jesus told Pilate, his kingdom would not come from the world system of empires. The kingdom of the Son of Man would not be based upon the coercive power of the beasts but upon the cosuffering love of a new humanity formed around Messiah.

Caiaphas didn't believe such a kingdom *had* come, and Pilate didn't believe such a kingdom *could* come. The question is, do *we*? Do we believe that Jesus is the Son of Man who has been given dominion over the nations and has established a new kind of rule? Or do we in effect say, "Oh, someday the Son of Man will reign, but not now, and in the meantime, let's trust Caesar to keep running the show"?

Why is Luke so careful to mention a cloud in his account of Jesus's ascension (Acts 1:9)? Luke hopes we will connect the dots and recognize that in his death, resurrection, and ascension, Jesus has inaugurated the reign of Daniel's Son of Man over all peoples, nations, and languages. Which is exactly the gospel that the apostles preached throughout the book of Acts! But do we believe that gospel? Do we believe that Jesus really is reigning over the nations? Or have we reduced Jesus's role to that of a personal Savior who presides only in the hearts of believers? If Jesus is relegated to the hyperspiritualized role of personal Savior, then we are free to pledge our political allegiance to the latest incarnation of empire. This is why Christians from the days of Constantine onward have been so pliable in the hands of beasts. We should think deeply upon the fact that the Nazi blitzkriegs were waged by baptized soldiers. Had the church held to pre-Constantine convictions, Hitler would never have gotten off the ground. Before we appeal to Hitler as the ultimate argument against Christian nonviolence, we first have to ask how Hitler was able to amass a following of Christians in the first place. After all, it wasn't atheists and pagans who formed the German Christian movement that lent support to Hitler in the 1930s.

During his final week in Jerusalem, Jesus spoke repeatedly about the coming of the Son of Man. And whereas I fully affirm that Jesus will "come again to judge the living and dead," I also believe that most of what Jesus is talking about in his Olivet discourse and his "coming of the Son of Man" parables has to do primarily with the coming of the kingdom of God inaugurated through his death and resurrection. So while we acknowledge that the reign of God is obviously not yet fully seen and that we await the coming again of Christ, we dare not say the kingdom of God has not come. What I'm trying to say is that Jesus *is* Lord. Today. Right now. For real. Jesus will appear for the final judgment, but he is *already* ruling and judging the nations in righteousness. We may prefer to opt for one of the dualistic options of either liberal utopianism or conservative dispensationalism, but the truth is we must live in the tension of the now and not yet. Jesus is *now* reigning over the nations, but we do *not yet* see the fullness of a world made right.

In Matthew 25, just a few days before his crucifixion and resurrection, Jesus gives a series of parables about the coming of the Son of Man. (He doesn't speak of this as a "second" coming.) Jesus first gives the parable of the bridesmaids, then the parable of the talents, and finally the parable of the sheep and goats. Jesus began the sheep and goats parable like this: "When the Son of Man comes in his glory, and all the angels with him, then he will sit on the throne of his glory" (Matt. 25:31). As hard as it may seem, try to resist automatically turning this into "When the Son of Man comes for the *second* time ..." No. Jesus was obviously working from Daniel 7. He spoke of the Son of Man's coming to a glorious throne and judging the nations—just like Daniel described. This is what Jesus told Caiaphas (and Pilate in a different way) was happening right then. And we should believe what Jesus confessed before Caiaphas and Pilate—that he is the Son of Man, that he is the world's true King. As Christians we confess that Jesus has ascended to the right hand of the throne of God in the heavens. This was a theme the apostles emphasized repeatedly. But what is Jesus doing at the right hand of God? Twiddling his thumbs? Biding his time? Idly waiting? No. He is ruling and judging the nations. Of course this is a mystery; I don't pretend that I am able to explain it all, but there is a sense in which the death, resurrection, and ascension of Jesus Christ has inaugurated a new justice in the earth, and nations that run headlong against the righteousness of God eventually fall into fiery judgment ... *now!* Whether it's Imperial Rome or Nazi Germany, nations cannot forever oppose the righteousness of God without falling into a fiery hell "prepared for the devil and his angels." The American colonies and nation practiced, for over two centuries, the most brutal form of slavery the world has ever known—until it was thrown into the hell of a civil war that claimed the lives of three quarters of a million people.

Yes, I believe in a personal judgment—"For all of us must appear before the judgment seat of Christ, so that each may receive recompense for what has been done in the body, whether good or evil" (2 Cor. 5:10). But I don't think this is what Jesus was particularly talking about in his parable of the sheep and goats. Jesus spoke of nations judged, not individuals. And the criterion for judgment has nothing to do with "receiving Jesus as Savior" but with the treatment of the underclass with whom Jesus claimed a particular solidarity.

When the Son of Man judges the nations, he divides them into sheep and goats. Interestingly, this division is not based on praying a sinner's prayer or getting saved or saying one is a Christian, but on the treatment of certain people. If you want to say this parable is not really about the judgment of nations but about the judgment of individuals, you are left with the problem that the criterion for judgment has nothing to do with "getting saved" or "receiving Jesus as your personal Savior." In other words, you are going to have a really hard time getting Jesus's parable of the sheep and goats to line up with a four-spiritual-laws view of personal salvation. It seems clear that the easiest way to make sense of this parable is to view it as the establishment of the new criterion for judgment for the nations that begins with the coming of the Son of Man—the thing that Jesus told Caiaphas he would see "from now on."

So how does Jesus judge or evaluate nations? What criteria does he use? When we evaluate nations, we tend to do so on the basis of wealth and power—Gross Domestic Product, standard of living, strength of the economy, strength of the military. But this is not the criterion Jesus uses to judge the nations as he sits upon his glorious throne. Jesus judges nations on how well they care for four kinds of people:

> **The Poor.** "I was hungry and you gave me food, I was thirsty and you gave me something to drink … I was naked and you gave me clothing."

> **The Sick.** "I was sick and you took care of me."

> **The Immigrant.** "I was a stranger and you welcomed me."

> **The Prisoner.** "I was in prison and you visited me." (Matt. 25:35–36)

In political conversation these days, we hear a lot about "right" and "left." People have a lot of passion about these teams, but I have no allegiance to either the political right or the political left for this simple reason: Jesus has his own right and left! In the Jesus right-left divide, you definitely want to be on the right. (The goats on the left are sent away into the hell prepared for the devil and his angels!) But what does it mean to belong to the true "religious right"? What does it mean to be a "sheep" nation judged to be on the right side of Jesus and blessed by God? It means to be a nation that cares for the poor, cares for the sick, welcomes the immigrant, and practices humane treatment of its prisoners. We can argue about how this is best to be done, but that these are the priorities of Christ is beyond dispute. These values reflect the politics of Jesus. These are the political priorities that flow from the Sermon on the Mount. These are the things that the Son of Man cares about. These are the issues that have priority in the administration of the King of Kings and the Lord of Lords. The poor, the sick, the immigrant, the prisoner. Conniving politicians may say, "It's the economy, stupid," but Jesus says, "No. It's how you care for the indigent and infirm; it's how you treat the immigrant and imprisoned."

Nations may choose to ignore these priorities, choosing instead to emphasize economic and military superiority, but eventually judgment will cause these superpowers to come crashing down. With the resurrection of the Son of God, the world changed. There's a new charter. A new divine law. Ever since the Son of God refounded the world at the cross and called humanity to organize itself around an axis of love expressed in mercy and forgiveness, a new moral law has been established in the cosmos that will not allow nations to forever oppose the will of God. And as the Hebrew prophets first began to reveal so long ago, the living God possesses a deep bias for the underclass and will judge nations accordingly. The death, resurrection, and ascension of our Lord has given the world a new ultimate reality—love for God expressed as love for neighbor and enemy. Any other agenda is idolatry. Babylon is still among us, but Babylon is always falling. The new gravity of grace will not allow modern Babylons to stand for long. Winning the game, being a superpower, having the biggest army or the most robust economy is not what matters. Not anymore. What matters now is love and mercy, especially for the weak, the disadvantaged, and the marginalized. As we organize ourselves into nations and states, if we do not act in concert with the new ultimate reality, we eventually find ourselves suffering the self-inflicted destruction that is the fate of the devil and his angels. Ever since Calvary the devil is being judged and cast out. Nations who continue to follow the cross-shamed ways of power, greed, and violence will share the devil's fate. Actually, Isaiah the prophet saw this long ago.

When asked to identify the origin of Satan, we are commonly directed to Isaiah 14. This is the passage where the king of Babylon is called Lucifer (Day Star) and described as "fallen from heaven" for coveting the throne of God. But what should be readily apparent is that Isaiah is giving us a prophetic critique of empire by using the king of Babylon as a personification for the whole imperial project. This is quite clear from a careful reading of the text.

> When the LORD has given you rest from your pain
> and turmoil and the hard service with which you
> were made to serve, you will take up this taunt
> against the king of Babylon:
>
> How the oppressor has ceased!
>   How his insolence is ceased!
> The LORD has broken the staff of the wicked,
>   the scepter of rulers,

that struck down the peoples in wrath
    with unceasing blows,
that ruled the nations in anger
    with unrelenting persecution.
The whole earth is at rest and quiet;
    they break forth into singing.
The cypresses exult over you,
    the cedars of Lebanon, saying,
"Since you were laid low,
    no one comes to cut us down."
Sheol beneath is stirred up
    to meet you when you come;
it rouses the shades to greet you,
    all who were leaders of the earth;
it raises from their thrones
    all who were kings of the nations.
All of them will speak
    and say to you:
"You too have become as weak as we!
    You have become like us!"
Your pomp is brought down to Sheol,
    and the sound of your harps;
maggots are the bed beneath you,
    and worms are your covering.

How you have fallen from Heaven,
    O Day Star, son of Dawn!
How you are cut down to the ground,

you who laid the nations low!
You said in your heart,
    "I will ascend to heaven;
I will raise my throne
    above the stars of God;
I will sit on the mount of assembly
    on the heights of Zaphon;
I will ascend to the tops of the clouds,
    I will make myself like the Most High."
But you are brought down to Sheol,
    to the depths of the Pit.
Those who see you will stare at you,
    and ponder over you:
"Is this the man who made the earth tremble,
    who shook kingdoms,
who made the world like a desert
    and overthrew its cities,
    who would not let his prisoners go home?"
All the kings of the nations lie in glory,
    each in his own tomb;
but you are cast out, away from your grave,
    like loathsome carrion,
clothed with the dead, those pierced by the sword,
    who go down to the stones of the Pit,
    like a corpse trampled underfoot.
You will not be joined with them in burial,
    Because you have destroyed your land,
    because you have killed your people.

> May the descendants of evildoers
>> nevermore be named!
> Prepare slaughter for his sons
>> because of the guilt of their father.
> Let them never rise to possess the earth
>> or cover the face of the world with cities. (Isa.
>> 14:3–21)

Throughout Scripture, and especially in the book of Revelation, Babylon remains a prophetic symbol of empires closely associated with the satanic. Biblically understood, empires are rich and powerful nations that believe they have a right to rule other nations and a manifest destiny to shape the world according to their agenda. But the prophets insist that God regards this as outrageous arrogance and a transgression upon his own sovereignty. The apostles tell us that what empires claim for themselves, God promises to his Son. God is forever opposed to empires. God loves nations and delights in their rich diversity, but God hates empires. Empires produce a pseudo-peace—a Pax Romana—but it is a peace that inevitably leads to war. Imperial dominance of a superpower nation over lesser nations incites resentment and retaliation leading to violence and war. The imperial-satanic project is always destined to fall. Thus the prophets continually cry, "Babylon is fallen, is fallen!" Through the animosity they engender among other nations, empires sow the seeds for their own eventual destruction. The prophets identify this as the judgment of God.

In Isaiah's taunt of Babylon we discover a number of the characteristics of empire. For example, they aggressively seek to rule other nations. Empires are arrogant in their environmental degradation—they view the earth as theirs and not the Lord's. Because of their paranoia and cruelty, they hold prisoners indefinitely. Empires practice the propaganda of calling destruction *peace*. Isaiah says Babylon made the world like a desert and overthrew its cities. Many centuries later the Roman historian Tacitus would record the British chieftain Calgacus as saying, "Rome makes a desert and calls it peace." I'm quite sure Calgacus never read Isaiah, but they were saying the same thing about the propaganda of empires. Empires believe in their own exceptionalism but end up being cut down to size, becoming like all the other nations. The real problem with empires is the hubris that impels them to impinge upon the sovereignty of God by seeking to rule other nations. This is condemned by the prophet as seeking to be like God. Empires want to raise their thrones (national sovereignty) to a level reserved for God. This is the essence and a primary origin of the satanic. In the end all empires have an expiration date. God decrees their demise lest they "rise to possess the earth or cover the face of the earth with cities." Babylon and New Jerusalem seek the same thing, but they go about it in completely different ways—one is beastly, the other is lamblike.

Lucifer (the king of Babylon) and his nation being thrust down to Sheol in Isaiah's taunt should probably be understood as largely the same thing as the goat nations joining the devil and his angels in Gehenna in Jesus's parable of the sheep and the goats. Babylon does not prioritize care for the poor and sick; Babylon does not welcome the immigrant; Babylon does not treat its prisoners humanely. So in both Isaiah's taunt and Jesus's parable, Babylon's fate was the fiery pit. Babylon continues to tell itself that if its economy and military are strong enough, it can guarantee its security. But Jesus said this is not so. With the coming of the Son of Man before the Ancient of Days, the nations who continue to act with imperial arrogance instead of human compassion are doomed to destruction.

The new moral law of love for neighbor and enemy that fully entered the world through the life and teaching, the death and resurrection of Jesus Christ make it impossible for rich and powerful nations to claim a divine right for dominance or a manifest destiny of exceptionalism. The kind of entitlement the Pharaohs and Caesars were for centuries able to claim for their empires has now been shamed by Christ and can never endure long. Greatness, and even security, is not found in wealth and might but in compassion and mercy. Just as Jesus called his followers to be great by serving one another, he also calls the nations to the same ethic. The nations who resist the ethic are inevitably hurtling toward their own destruction.

So politically I call for my nation to prioritize caring for the poor, the sick, the immigrant, and the imprisoned, and to renounce an ambition to dominate the world economically or militarily. I do this in the name of Jesus. I pledge no allegiance to elephants or donkeys, only to the Lamb. These are my politics for the simple reason that they are clearly the politics of Jesus. *Jesus says so!* Are you good with that? Or do your partisan political allegiances make it hard for you to accept the politics of Jesus? If so, you have some thinking to do.

CHAPTER 8

A FAREWELL TO MARS

The title of the book is *A Farewell to Arms* and except for three years there has been war of some kind almost ever since it has been written. Some people used to say, why is the man so preoccupied and obsessed with war, and now, since 1933 perhaps it is clear why a writer should be interested in the constant, bullying, murderous, slovenly crime of war. Having been to too many of them, I am sure that I am prejudiced, and I hope that I am very prejudiced. But it is the considered belief of the writer of this book that wars are fought by the finest people that there are, or just say people, although, the closer you are to where they are fighting, the finer people you meet; but they are made, provoked and initiated by straight economic rivalries and by swine that stand to profit from them.[1]

—Ernest Hemingway, *A Farewell to Arms*

Mars. The red planet. Blood red. The god of arms. The god of war. Men are from Mars. Or so we're told. Mars was born as Ares, the Greek god of war—a cruel god often treated with contempt in Greek mythology. But once the Greek god of war was adopted and renamed by the Romans centuries later, Mars was reborn with a positive public image. If Ares was feared and held in contempt, Mars was beloved and celebrated. A farewell to Ares and a welcome to Mars. Mars, depicted in sculpture with a great spear in hand, was a favorite god whose temples proliferated throughout the empire. In Roman mythology Mars was the father of the Roman people— the father of Romulus and Remus. In Roman political theory Mars was the bringer of peace—peace by war. The euphemistic peace that was the tyranny of the Pax Romana was the achievement of an empire that venerated war and worshipped Mars.

Of course that was all a very long time ago. The stuff of history. Who worships Mars anymore? Today, Roman statues of Mars are found only in museums. I've never heard anyone invoke the name of Mars in prayer. So Mars is a has-been god, right? Hardly. Mars is still very much with us (though living under an assumed name). Wherever war is given sanctity in the name of God, Mars is there. Wherever military might is wedded with religious rhetoric, Mars is there. Wherever the symbols of faith morph into the emblems of war, Mars is there. Mars is not dead. Mars lives on. Mars is alive and well in our day. I've even been to a modern temple of Mars.

I was speaking at a church in Colorado Springs and someone suggested that Peri and I visit the nearby Air Force Academy. They thought we might be interested in seeing the controversial Cadet

Chapel—a National Historic Landmark that receives more than a million visitors each year. So we went. The exterior architecture of the modernistic chapel resembles seventeen fighter jets pointed upward forming seventeen spires that reach 150 feet into the air. I was aware of this controversial exterior design (fighter jets forming a Christian chapel!), but I knew nothing about the interior. We parked in the visitors lot and strolled across the beautiful grounds of the academy to the Cadet Chapel. The Air Force Academy is home to four thousand of America's brightest and best students. Admission standards are extremely high. The cadets are young people who have been honor students, valedictorians, high school quarterbacks, class presidents, and the like—high-achieving, civic-minded leaders in their communities. Most receive a nomination for admission from their congressman. They are among the best of the best. A visitor senses the commitment to excellence that pervades the Air Force Academy.

When we arrived at the chapel, a sign near the entrance read, "Our most recognized landmark, soaring 150 feet toward the Colorado sky, the Air Force Academy Cadet Chapel is the iconic structure for the United States Air Force Academy." After taking a few pictures of the fighter-jet-themed exterior, which I can only describe as brutal architecture, we entered the main Protestant chapel—a large vaulted sanctuary that can seat twelve hundred worshippers. Inside there were stained-glass windows, wooden pews, a communion table, a pulpit, Bibles, and hymnals. It was obviously intended as a Christian house of worship. But what arrested my attention the moment I entered was the nearly fifty-foot "cross" that hung above the altar. I put the word in quotes because though it hung where a cross would be expected and it was no doubt intended to remind the worshipper of a cross, it wasn't a cross. It was a sword. This enormous aluminum "cross" had a propeller for a hilt and a metal blade with a central ridge and a tapered point. It was *not* a cross. It was a *sword*! I was stunned. Angry even. The cross of Christ had been replaced by a sword of war. This is no insignificant thing. Peri was upset and wanted to leave. As we drove away from the Air Force Academy, I told her, "That was no Christian chapel; that was a temple of Mars."

What I saw in the Cadet Chapel was a fusion of iconography—Christian symbols wedded with militaristic emblems. It was Constantine placing Christian symbols on implements of war all over again. Fighter jets forming a house of Christian worship. Mars mashed-up with Jesus. The god of war subsuming the Prince of Peace. That's what I saw. A cross transformed into a sword. The irony is deep. Originally the Roman cross *was* a weapon of war. The Romans used crucifixion as a form of psychological warfare to intimidate the population into compliance with the empire. Crucifixion was a means of torture and execution reserved for insurrectionists and rebellious slaves—those who threatened the security of the empire. Jesus lived his whole life under the ominous shadow of a Roman cross. From the beginning of his ministry, Jesus knew his life would end with an ignominious death upon a Roman cross. Jesus knew he would die on the supreme symbol of Roman military might. A Roman cross was where Jesus would die for the sins of the world—sins that were sinned into him with violence by the principalities and powers. The cross was also the place where Jesus would refound the world. Instead of being arranged around an axis of power enforced by violence, at the cross Jesus rearranged the world around an axis of love expressed in forgiveness. Jesus would not torture and kill his enemies; he would be tortured and killed ... and forgive his enemies. Jesus subverted the cross. The Roman Empire used the cross to communicate how ruthlessly it would eliminate its enemies. Jesus used the cross to communicate that there was no one to be eliminated. Forgiveness, not elimination, is the message of the Christian cross. But what is the message of the cross-turned-sword in the modern-day temple of Mars?

The most radical thing about the Christian life is that Jesus calls us to take up our own cross and follow his example. Why are followers of Christ called to carry their own cross? So we can bring about righteousness by torturing and killing our enemies? No! Jesus has transformed the cross. Christians carry the cross because we are willing, at any moment, to imitate our Lord by dying at the hands of our enemies rather than perpetuating the cycle of fear and violence. This was how Jesus subverted a Roman military implement and turned it into the definitive symbol of the Christian faith. Because of Christ and his resurrection, the Roman cross no longer represents torture and death. It now represents love and forgiveness. Jesus used an implement of violence and war to offer the world an alternative to violence and war. We are not safe. But we are saved.

So what does the sword-cum-cross in the Air Force Academy Cadet Chapel mean? What is its message? Is it intended to communicate to the worshipper that as Christians we are willing to lay down our lives and die by the sword of our enemy in imitation of our Lord? Of course not! It means just the opposite. It is intended to communicate to the worshipper that Christ himself blesses the weapons we wield and the wars we wage. The symbolic message is this: following Christ and waging war are completely compatible. Or perhaps even this: the sword saves the world. Good guys killing bad guys redeems the world. Eliminating evil people can eliminate evil. But it's all a lie. A terrible, pernicious lie. A satanic lie. It is the unmaking of the cross. It's a faith undone.

Some will wonder if I am saying a Christian cannot enlist in the armed forces or enroll in a military academy. That is not my point. My point is that when a military academy builds a chapel out of fighter jets and replaces the cross with a sword, it is not for the worship of Christ but for the worship of Mars—even if that's not consciously acknowledged. That's what I'm saying. Nevertheless, I agree with Lee Camp when he reminds us:

> Appealing to the authority of Jesus, the early church generally believed its vocation did not entail waging the wars of empires, no matter how just. They had a different vocation, a different politics, namely, to embody the peaceable reign of God that had been inaugurated in Jesus of Nazareth, who himself incarnated the peaceable will of God, loving even unto death, and triumphing over the powers in his shameful crucifixion. The "wisdom of God" was foolishness to the world but was nonetheless the power unto the saving of the world. It was patient, suffering love, not justifiable war that would save the world.[2]

Isaiah had a dream, a God-inspired dream. Isaiah was a poet, a God-intoxicated poet. He had a Messianic dream that he turned into a prophetic poem. It goes like this:

> In days to come
>> the mountain of the LORD's house
> shall be established as the highest of the mountains,
>> and shall be raised above the hills;
> all the nations shall stream to it.
>> Many peoples shall come and say,
> "Come, let us go up to the mountain of the LORD,
>> to the house of the God of Jacob;
> that he may teach us his ways
>> and that we may walk in his paths."
> For out of Zion shall go forth instruction,
>> and the word of the LORD from Jerusalem.
> He shall judge between the nations,
>> and shall arbitrate for many peoples;
> they shall beat their swords into plowshares,
>> and their spears into pruning hooks;
> nation shall not lift up sword against nation,
>> neither shall they learn war any more. (Isa. 2:2–4)

Swords turned into plowshares, spears into pruning hooks. Tanks turned into tractors, missile silos into grain silos. The study of war abandoned for learning the ways of the Lord. Instead of academies where we learn to make war, there will be universities where we learn to wage peace. The cynic will laugh (for lack of imagination), but this is Isaiah's vision. And every Christmas we borrow another of Isaiah's poems to celebrate the birth of the Child who makes these dreams come true.

> The people who walked in darkness
>   have seen a great light;
> those who live in a land of deep darkness—
>   on them light has shined ...
> For all the boots of the tramping warriors
>   and all the garments rolled in blood
>   shall be burned as fuel for fire.
> For a child has been born for us,
>   a son given to us;
> authority rests on his shoulders;
>   and he is named
> Wonderful Counselor, Mighty God,
>   Everlasting Father, Prince of Peace.
> His authority shall grow continually,
>   and there shall be endless peace
> for the throne of David and his kingdom.
>   He will establish and uphold it
> with justice and with righteousness
>   from this time onward and forevermore. (Isa.
>   9:2, 5–7)

Isaiah, in his prophetic poems, frames the Messianic hope like this: A Prince of Peace will establish a new kind of government, a government characterized by ever-increasing peace. Weapons of war will be transformed into instruments of agriculture. At last the nations will find their way out of the darkness of endless war into the light of God's enduring peace. This is Isaiah's hope.

Christians take Isaiah's hope and make a daring claim: Jesus *is* that Prince of Peace. Jesus *is* the one who makes Isaiah's dreams come true. From the day of Pentecost to the present, this is what Christians have claimed. But then a doom-obsessed dispensationalist performs an eschatological sleight of hand and takes the hope away from us. On one hand, they admit that Jesus is the Prince of Peace who has come, but on the other hand, they say his peace is not for now ... it's only for when Jesus comes back again. Bait and switch. Yes, swords are to become plowshares ... but not today. For now plowshares become swords; in our day, it's war, war, war! They abuse Jesus's prediction of the destruction of Jerusalem in the first century by always applying it to the latest contemporary geopolitical events. They replace the hope of peace with an anticipation of war! They find a way to make war a hopeful sign. Think about that for a moment! And here is the worst irony: It was precisely because Jerusalem failed to recognize Jesus as Isaiah's Prince of Peace *right there and then* that they rushed headlong into the war that ended with their own destruction!

End-time prophecy experts keep trying to force the same mistake on us in our day. We should refuse. I am a conscientious objector to the doom-obsessed, hyperviolent, war-must-come, pillage-the-Bible-for-the-worst-we-can-find eschatology of Hal Lindsey and his tribe. We must reject that kind of warmongering misinterpretation of Scripture. Jesus doesn't call us to give a prophetic interpretation to the latest war and rumor of war. Jesus calls us to be peacemakers and lead the way out of the darkness of retributive violence into the light of Christian reconciliation. But we haven't done a very good job of it. I suppose I shouldn't get so upset about a military academy beating a cross into a sword when Christian interpreters have been doing the same thing since the days of Constantine. But it's time we stopped doing it. It's time we started believing what we say every Christmas—the Prince of Peace has come!

Isaiah says that in the last days, the nations will come to Mount Zion and learn the peaceful ways of the Lord. That's when weapons of war will become implements of agriculture. Well, let's believe it! The apostle Peter said on the day of Pentecost that the last days have arrived (Acts 2:14ff). The writer of Hebrews said that in Christ we have come to Mount Zion (Heb. 12:22ff). Obviously, with the passing of two thousand years, it should be clear that Peter didn't mean the end of time was imminent; rather he meant exactly what Jesus himself had been saying—that the waiting was over, the time was fulfilled, and all that the prophets had foretold was coming to pass in the present. The writer of Hebrews means that what Isaiah and the other Hebrew prophets had described as the nations flowing to Mount Zion to learn the way of peace has been inaugurated with the death, burial, and resurrection of Christ. Let me say it clearly: if you are waiting for something to happen before you beat your sword into a plowshare and your spear into a pruning hook, you can stop waiting! If you confess that Jesus is the Prince of Peace foretold by the prophets, you can start being a peacemaker—today! You don't need to wait for anything else. You *shouldn't* wait for anything else!

As followers of the Prince of Peace, are we ready to bid farewell to Mars? We must be. The god of war has had his day. His day ended on the first Easter. In his death and resurrection, Christ abolished war. Christ made it clear on the cross that war will no longer be the way the world is transformed. The cross exposes the use of violent force as a shameful practice to be renounced. Yes, Christ has abolished war. The King of Kings won his kingdom without war. Jesus proved there is another way. Jesus *is* the other way. The question "What are you willing to die for?" is not the same question as "What are you willing to kill for?" Jesus was willing to die for that which he was unwilling to kill for. Jesus won his kingdom by dying, not killing. Ruling the world by killing was buried with Christ. When Christ was raised on the third day, he did not resurrect war. With his resurrection the world is given a new trajectory, an eschatology toward peace.

> With his appearance the eschatological Israel is beginning: as a truly human society coming entirely from God and no longer built on violence, but rather nonviolence even if that should mean death. But it is precisely in this that its power is revealed. It will be mightier than the strength of all the great powers and world empires.[3]

War is a thing of the past. War is anachronistic. War is regression. War is a pledge of fealty to a bloody past. War is a sacrament offered to Mars. War is a repudiation of the lordship of Christ. The followers of Christ must lead the way in imagining something better than war. Who are the post-Hiroshima dreamers who dared to imagine a world beyond war? John Lennon? Perhaps. But what about someone far removed from the 1960s counterculture? Someone like President Dwight D. Eisenhower. In 1953, early in his presidency, Eisenhower warned:

> Every gun that is made, every warship launched, every rocket fired, signifies, in the final sense, a theft from those who hunger and are not fed, those who are cold and are not clothed … The cost of one modern heavy bomber is this: a modern brick school in more than 30 cities. It is two electric power plants, each serving a town of 60,000 population. It is two fine, fully equipped hospitals. It is some 50 miles of concrete highway. We pay for a single fighter plane with a half million bushels of wheat. We pay for a single destroyer with new homes that could have housed more than 8,000 people.[4]

President Eisenhower dreamed Isaiah's dream. The general who had been the Supreme Allied Commander during World War II dared to dream of heavy bombers becoming brick schools, fighter planes becoming bushels of wheat, warships becoming new houses for thousands.

And what should 1950s Bible-believing American Christians have done? They should have shouted, "Amen, Mr. President! Let us lead the way. The Jesus way. The way the Prince of Peace taught in the Sermon on the Mount." But that didn't happen. Instead, those most vociferous about being a Christian nation were busy scouring the book of Revelation to prove that Khrushchev was the antichrist. They were the biggest cheerleaders for the Cold War arms race. They were the loudest voices calling for plowshares to be turned into swords.

A decade later this led American evangelicals to be among the strongest supporters of the Vietnam War. The argument was that we had to combat atheistic communism by stopping its spread in Southeast Asia—if not, the whole world would fall to Communism. The "domino theory." So young American men were sent to fight and die in a Vietnamese civil war. This madness somehow made sense to most evangelical Christians. For the cause of Christ to prosper in the world, seven million tons of bombs had to be dropped on villages in Southeast Asia. (The newly graduated cadets who prayed in the sword-adorned academy chapel were the pilots and bombardiers doing the bidding of men behind desks in Washington, DC.) But how did that work out? Fifty-eight thousand Americans died in Vietnam. The war was lost. Vietnam became communist. Yet somehow the dominos did not fall. The hawks were wrong. Instead, Soviet Bloc communism ran out of steam and collapsed under its own weight a couple of decades later. The fall of communism had more to do with prayer meetings in Poland than bombs dropped on Cambodia. War is, among other things, impatience.

War, as a legitimate means of shaping the world, died with Christ on Good Friday. Jesus refuted the war option when he told Peter to put up his sword. Killing in order to liberate Jesus and his followers from the violent injustice of Caiaphas, Herod, and Pilate would have been a just war—but Jesus refused to engage in a just war. He chose instead to bear witness to the truth, forgive, and die.

Jesus took the death of a world framed by war into his body and he and it both died together. Jesus was buried and with him was buried the old world devoted to sin and death. On the third day Jesus was raised and a new world was born. Of course the old world of death still lingers around us, but in the midst of it, the world to come is being born. The first person to meet Jesus on that first Easter Sunday was Mary Magdalene. She thought he was the gardener. She wasn't wrong. Jesus is a gardener—the true gardener, the gardener Adam was meant to be.

Jesus is the firstborn of the new humanity—a humanity of gardeners turning garbage dumps into gardens, swords into plowshares, war waging into peacemaking. The resurrection of Jesus is not just a happy ending to the gospel story; it is the dawn of a new creation. No one captures this idea better than G. K. Chesterton in the close of part one of his classic work, *The Everlasting Man*.

> On the third day the friends of Christ coming at daybreak to the place found the grave empty and the stone rolled away. In varying ways they realised the new wonder; but even they hardly realised that the world had died in the night. What they were looking at was the first day of a new creation, with a new heaven and a new earth; and in a semblance of the gardener God walked again in the garden, in the cool not of the evening but the dawn.[5]

On the evening of his resurrection Jesus appeared to his disciples in the upper room, saying, "Peace be with you." He showed them his

wounds and then said again, "Peace be with you" (John 20:19–21).
Peace is the first word of a new world. Having absorbed the sin and
death of Cain's violent civilization into his own body, Jesus carried it
away to Hades and on the third day rose again to speak a fresh new
word to the world of humankind—the word *peace*!

With the death, burial, and resurrection of Christ, the kingdom
of God has come—and it is a peaceable kingdom. It's time for the
lion to lay down with the lamb. War belongs to the previous age
governed by the satan. The age to come, inaugurated in Christ's resurrection, is an age where war is abolished, peace reigns, and spears
are set aside for pruning hooks.

Does everyone accept this? Of course not. That's why the
anachronism of war is still with us. But those who confess Christ
has been raised are to embody the reign of Christ here and now.
No more eschatological shenanigans where we keep pushing the
reign of Christ off until we've waged a few more wars. No! The Lion
of Judah has overcome the beasts of empire, and he's done so as a
slaughtered Lamb. Now we are called to follow the Lamb and give
incarnation to his ways of peace. We who believe that Christ has
risen have heard our Lord say, "Peace be with you. As the Father
sent me, so I send you" (John 20:21). What Jesus did to embody
the will of the Father on the cross was not just done on our behalf;
it was also done as the way we are to follow. Jesus did not renounce
the way of violence for the way of peace so that we could renounce
the way of peace for the way of violence. The long dark night of
mankind's addiction to violence has come to an end. The new day
of Messiah's peace has dawned, and we are called to be children of
the day. Do we dare?

Peri and I have been to a modern temple of Mars. We have seen a chapel designed to glorify the weapons of war. We have seen a cross turned into a sword. We know that the cadets who worship in that chapel are amongst the finest young men and women in America. They are bright, courageous, disciplined, and loyal. They are modern-day centurions. (It's worth noting that the five Roman centurions mentioned in the Gospels and Acts are all portrayed in a positive light.) But we also know that the gospel of peace is being obscured by a church that has long been more interested in serving as a chaplain to its host superpower than embarking about the risky path of following Jesus as the Prince of Peace. And even that in 1959, a fighter-jet–themed chapel with a sword for a cross that was constructed at a military academy is not really the fault of the architect and those who envisioned the project. It's the fault of the church. The whole church. The post-Constantine church that got into bed with empires. Greek Orthodox, Roman Catholics, British Anglicans, German Lutherans, American Evangelicals have all done it. I've done it. I've prayed war prayers and preached war sermons. I've helped perpetuate idolatrous allegiance to nationalism, violence, and war. I'm in no place to point a finger. For that matter I'm not really interested in blaming the church of the fourth century for their now obvious mistake. Perhaps it was inevitable. Gerhard Lohfink seems to think so.

> The development toward an imperial Church and
> finally toward a state religion was almost a matter of
> necessity, given the constellation of late antiquity.
> Perhaps the Church had to take that road. It was

a grandiose attempt to create a Christian "empire" and thus to unite faith, life, and culture.

Only a careful look at the people of God in the Old Testament, their experiment with the state and the collapse of the experiment, could have preserved the Church from repeating the old mistake. But it was not possible in late antiquity or in the Middle Ages for people to read the Old Testament so analytically. Political theology was, instead, enraptured with David and Solomon. Only the history of the modern era shattered the dream.

Today the experiment is truly at an end and can never be resumed.[6]

Gerhard Lohfink is right. Experimentation with building a Christian empire through the apparatus of the state, including waging war, was, perhaps, inevitable—but that experiment has come to an end. The experiment was a disaster. We now know better. We can no longer pretend that the organized, state-sponsored killing that is war is compatible with the kingdom of Christ. Jesus did not come to help us win our wars—no matter what Constantine thought. Jesus came to lead us out of the dark and demonic world of war into the light of his peaceable kingdom. Did it require seventeen centuries for us to learn this lesson? I don't know. I do know that on August 6, 1945, the world crossed a threshold. Human capacity for killing is now totalized. We can kill the whole world if we want to. Will we continue to believe the lie that we have to kill the world in order to save it? This is the lie Cain told himself. In a mystical sense Cain killed the world when he killed his brother. Then he built the city of human civilization upon the lie that we can do good by killing. The cherished lie. The memorialized lie. The Mars lie. The lie that we save the world by killing it. We tell ourselves the lie: "We are the good guys. They are the bad guys. If we kill them, we will save the world." That's Cain's logic. Of course Cain couldn't really kill the whole world with his club. But we can. We have a club that can kill the whole world ... though they tell me the cockroaches might survive.

Yet there is hope. In Christ we have the possibility of a better world. The church should work for this better world, refusing to collude with Death and Company. If there were ever a time when the world needed a people who really believe in Jesus and his radical ideas of love, forgiveness, and peace, and believe them enough to live them and, if need be, die for them, that time is ...

NOW!

After our surreal visit to the "temple of Mars" at the Air Force Academy, Peri and I were walking through the Denver airport when I noticed a mural. It was Leo Tanguma's "The Children of the World Dream of Peace." I had walked past that mural dozens of times and somehow never noticed it. The mural is an artistic celebration of Isaiah's hopeful dream that some day peace will prevail, that the plow really can replace the sword, that children can inherit a world without war. In the colorful mural, children dressed in native folk costume and paired with their historic national enemies are bringing swords to the center of the mural where they are being beaten into plowshares. Pakistanis and Indians. Iraqis and Iranians. Chinese and Tibetans. Americans and Russians. Israelis and Palestinians. The children have wrapped swords in their national flags, and together, they carry the swords to where they will be transformed into plowshares. At the bottom of the mural lies a broken statue of a grotesque figure of war clutching a broken gun. Next to the fallen statue is a cracked tombstone bearing the inscription: "War. Violence. Hate." Curling across the top of the mural is a banner that has the word *peace* in twelve languages. This was Isaiah's dream. The dream Christians claim is coming true in Christ. For years I had ignored this mural of peace in the Denver airport. I simply had not seen it. Just like I had for years ignored the gospel of peace in my life and preaching. I simply had not seen it. I was blind. But I'm beginning to see, at last I am waking up—waking up just in time to try and make a difference for the world of my children's children. I suppose it is for them I have written this book.

I know what the cynics will say. I know how the scoffers will sneer. I know the non-dreamers believing only in the brutal ways of force will laugh me off as impossibly naive. But I don't care. I've grown immune to their strain of unbelief. I've turned a corner. I believe that what Isaiah dreamed of, Jesus died for. I believe that what Isaiah said would come to pass in the last days, Jesus inaugurated in his resurrection. I've caught a glimpse of the better world that can be—a world that Jesus came to give and continues to offer us. I believe the world of peace is possible in Christ. I won't let the doomsday preppers with their Armageddon obsession talk me out of it. Jesus has already spoken the first word of a new world—the word *peace*. So things have changed. I have changed. I've prayed my last war prayer and preached my last war sermon. I've given up bellicose flag waving and singing lustily about bombs bursting in air. I've bid a final farewell to Mars. From now on I follow the Prince of Peace. I know others will come with me. Maybe you will be one of them. I hope so.

CHAPTER 9

US AND THEM

There is no them; there is only us.

NOTES

CHAPTER 1—"THAT PREACHER OF PEACE"

1 Mikhail Afanas'evich Bulgakov, *The Master and Margarita* (New York: Everyman's Library, 1992), 29–30.

2 Miroslav Volf, *Exclusion and Embrace* (Nashville: Abingdon Press, 1996), 276.

3 Bulgakov, *The Master*, 36.

4 Walter Brueggemann, *The Prophetic Imagination, 2nd Edition* (Minneapolis, MN: Augsburg Fortress, 2001), 40.

5 Fyodor Dostoevsky, *Demons*, trans. by Richard Pevear and Larissa Volokhonsky (New York: Random House, 1994), 251–52.

6 René Girard, *Things Hidden Since the Foundation of the World* (Stanford, CA: Stanford University Press, 1978), 197.

CHAPTER 2—REPAIRING THE WORLD

1 Emil Fackenheim, *To Mend the World: Foundations of Post Holocaust Jewish Thought* (Bloomington, IN: Indiana University Press, 1994), 213.

2 Acts 3:21; Romans 8:19–21; 1 Corinthians 15:24; Ephesians 1:20–23; Colossians 1:19–20.

3 Thomas Merton, *Raids on the Unspeakable* (New York: New Directions Publishing, 1966), 5.

4 David Bentley Hart, *Atheist Delusions: The Christian Revolution and Its Fashionable Enemies* (New Haven, CT: Yale University Press, 2010), 32–33.

CHAPTER 3—CHRIST AGAINST THE CROWD

1 Søren Kierkegaard, *Provocations: Spiritual Writings of Kierkegaard* (Maryknoll, NY: Orbis Books, 2003), 23.

2 Kierkegaard, *Provocations*, 23.

3 René Girard, *Sacrifice* (East Lansing, MI: Michigan State University Press, 2011), 72.

4 René Girard and James G. Williams, *The Girard Reader*, trans. by Jean-Michel Oughourlian (New York: Crossroad Publishing, 1996), 182.

5 Ecumenical Patriarch Bartholomew, *Encountering the Mystery: Understanding Orthodox Christianity Today* (New York: Doubleday, 2008), 210.

CHAPTER 4—IT'S HARD TO BELIEVE IN JESUS

1 Mark Twain, *The War Prayer* (New York: Harper Colophon, 1900).

2 Twain, *War Prayer*.

3 Twain, *War Prayer*.

4 Twain, *War Prayer*.

5 Twain, *War Prayer*.

6 John R. Cihak, "Love Alone Is Believable: Hans Urs von Balthasar's Apologetics," *Ignatius Insight*, accessed February 6, 2014, www.ignatiusinsight.com/features2005/jcihak_hubapol_may05.asp.

7 Will Willimon, "How Christian Leaders Have Changed Since 9/11," *Christianity Today*, September 2011, Vol. 55, No. 9, www.christianitytoday.com/ct/2011/september/howleaderschanged.html?start=5.

CHAPTER 5—FREEDOM'S JUST ANOTHER WORD FOR …

1 Bob Dylan, "Rainy Day Women #12 & 35," *Blonde on Blonde*, copyright © 1966 by Dwarf Music, renewed 1994 by Dwarf Music.

2 James Carroll, *Jerusalem, Jerusalem: How the Ancient City Ignited the Modern World* (New York: Houghton Mifflin, 2011), 17.

3 Fyodor Dostoevsky, *The Brothers Karamazov*, trans. Richard Pevear and Larissa Volokhonsky (New York: Farra, Straus, and Giroux: 1990), 313–14

4 Rowan Williams, *Christ on Trial: How the Gospel Unsettles Our Judgment* (Grand Rapids, MI: Eerdmans, 2003), 77.

5 David Bentley Hart, *The Beauty of the Infinite: The Aesthetics of Christian Truth* (Grand Rapids, MI: Eerdmans, 2003), 399.

6 Larry Norman, "The Great American Novel," *Only Visiting This Planet* © 1972 Air Studios.

CHAPTER 6—THE THINGS THAT MAKE FOR PEACE

1 Mark Twain, *Adventures of Huckleberry Finn* (Norwalk, CT: Easton Press, 1994), 291.

CHAPTER 7—CLOUDS, CHRIST, AND KINGDOM COME

1 Bob Dylan, "Political World," *Oh Mercy*, copyright © 1989 by Special Rider Music.

2 Trevin Wax, "From Word-Faith to the Church Fathers: A Conversation with Brian Zahnd," *Kingdom People*, June 28, 2012, http://thegospelcoalition.org/blogs/trevinwax/2012/06/28/from-word-faith-to-the-church-fathers-a-conversation-with-brian-zahnd/.

CHAPTER 8—A FAREWELL TO MARS

1 Ernest Hemingway, *A Farewell to Arms* (New York: Scribner, 2012), ix.

2 Lee C. Camp, *Who Is My Enemy? Questions American Christians Must Face about Islam—and Themselves* (Grand Rapids, MI: Brazo, 2011), 66.

3 Gehard Lohfink, *Does God Need the Church? Toward a Theology of the People of God* (Collegeville, MN: Liturgical Press, 1999), 179.

4 Aaron B. O'Connell, "The Permanent Militarization of America," *New York Times*, November 4, 2012, http://nyti.ms/WnWvo7.

5 G. K. Chesterton, *The Everlasting Man* (San Francisco: Ignatius Press, 1993), 213.

6 Lohfink, *Does God Need the Church?* 217–18.